the toilet
PAPERS

ken weber

The BOSTON
MILLS PRESS

DEDICATION

To U.S. astronaut Pete Conrad, the first man to go completely around the Earth while sitting on the john. (In 1973, aboard the Skylab space station, Conrad sat on the can for 90 minutes while the craft made one complete orbit of our planet, an accomplishment timed and verified by his fellow astronauts.)

Cataloging in Publication Data

Weber, K. J. (Kenneth Jerome), 1940–
        The toilet papers: wit, wisdom and wickedly funny stuff for reading in the john

ISBN 1-55046-308-X

1. Canadian wit and humor (English).*
I Title.

PS8595.E3246T64 1999   C818'.5402
99-931866-7
PR9199.3.W396T64 1999

Copyright © 1999 Ken Weber

03 02 01 00 99   1 2 3 4 5

Published in 1999 by
BOSTON MILLS PRESS
132 Main Street
Erin, Ontario N0B 1T0
Tel 519-833-2407
Fax 519-833-2195
e-mail books@boston-mills.on.ca
www.boston-mills.on.ca

An affiliate of
STODDART PUBLISHING CO. LIMITED
34 Lesmill Road
Toronto, Ontario, Canada
M3B 2T6
Tel 416-445-3333
Fax 416-445-5967
e-mail gdsinc@genpub.com

Distributed in Canada by
GENERAL DISTRIBUTION SERVICES
LIMITED
325 Humber College Boulevard
Toronto, Canada M9W 7C3
Orders 1-800-387-0141 Ontario &
        Quebec
Orders 1-800-387-0172 NW Ontario
        & other provinces
e-mail customer.service@ccmailgw.gen-
        pub.com
EDI Canadian Telebook 61150391

Distributed in the United States by
GENERAL DISTRIBUTION SERVICES INC.
85 River Rock Drive, Suite 202
Buffalo, New York 14207-2170
Toll-free 1-800-805-1083
°Toll-free fax 1-800-481-6207
e-mail gdsinc@genpub.com ·
www.genpub.com
PUBNET 6307949

Design by Mary Firth
Cover design by Gillian Stead
Printed in Canada

THE CANADA COUNCIL | LE CONSEIL DES ARTS
FOR THE ARTS | DU CANADA
SINCE 1957 | DEPUIS 1957

We acknowledge for their financial support of our publishing program the Canada Council, the Ontario Arts Council, and the Government of Canada through the Book Publishing Industry Development Program (BPIDP).

contents

emerge informed

In 1858 Hyman Lipman appeared at the patent office in Philadelphia with an application for an idea he'd developed. He was granted a patent for a pencil that had a piece of rubber glued onto its end. This was almost four decades after the first pencil factory was up and running in the U.S., and just under a century after erasers were first used in England. By this time, "lead" (actually, clay and graphite) pencils had been around for about three centuries. Sometimes it takes a while for human ingenuity to put two and two (or in this case, one and one) together!

A spell of hot weather officially becomes a heat wave after three or more consecutive days in which the temperature hits 32°C. If you're a Fahrenheiter, that's about 90°. Either way, it's hot.

Early in 1999, a directive was issued to the fingerprinting section of the Seattle Police Department, requiring that all members attend a class on how to sit down safely. The order was issued, according to the *Washington Monthly*, after two members of the section had fallen off of their chairs and injured themselves.

Hundreds of bad jokes had to be restructured in 1991 when the U.S. National Academy of Sciences published data showing that Spanish Fly really does work. On beetles. Specifically, on the fire-colored beetle. (If you are interested in pursuing this revelation further, guys hanging out in science bars refer to this particular beetle as *Neopyrochroa flabellata*. Spanish Fly is properly known as the chemical cantharidin.) The male beetle applies it to the female. But lest anyone reading this plans to push back the borders of scientific knowledge by trying a similar tactic on a human, be aware that cantharadin causes serious skin irritations on humans, most especially urogenital blistering.

From soccer we get the phrase "back to square one." In the days before TV, live radio broadcasts of soccer games in England were supported by a numbered grid plan of the soccer field, published in the BBC's *Radio Times*. Play by play commentators would refer to the grid to let listeners know where the action was taking place. In soccer, a team under pressure will frequently try to regroup and get a play started again by passing the ball back to its goalkeeper, who is always in square one.

 # not their finest hour

March 1947: A gunnery crew aboard the destroyer HMS *Saintes*, taking regular practice off Portsmouth, waited for the civilian tug *Buccaneer* to tow a target into range and then steam to safety. When the order came to fire, *Saintes* sank the *Buccaneer* in the first salvo. While everyone was busy rescuing the tug's skipper, the target caught a current flowing toward the Azores and was never seen again.

September 1996: It was a quiet day at the San Mateo County, California, sheriff's office, so when a 911 call came in from a pay phone two blocks away, an entire platoon of bored deputies tore out of the lot in response. In no time at all they screamed to a halt at the pay phone, where a somewhat dazed Maliu Mafua, 27, was holding the receiver. Mafua was wearing a shirt that read "Property of San Mateo County Jail." Seems he had meant to dial 411 for directory assistance, but numbers were never his strong suit. Interestingly, most of the jail authorities were not even aware that one of their scholars had escaped.

December 1759: The first (im)practical pair of roller skates were built and demonstrated by Joseph Merlin in the Belgian city of Huy. Merlin's day job was making violins, and he created a media event just before Christmas in 1759 by rolling into a costume party while playing one of his products. That part was effective. The party was the social high point of the year, and all Belgium's movers and shakers were there. Less effective were Merlin's skates. With no ball bearings, no swivels, and only two wheels on each skate — one behind the other in the center of the foot. After nailing down one hundred percent attention with his first stride, Merlin zigzagged across the room and crashed into a full-length mirror, breaking it, his violin, and his arm. (Roller skating did not become popular until 1884, after the invention of ball bearings. Merlin may have been a tad early.)

March 1978: Owing to a striking lack of publicity about the annual Arklow Music Festival, in County Wicklow, Ireland, only one choir, the Dublin Welsh Male Voice Choir, showed up to sing at the event. And they came in second in the competition. Seems the judges felt they should be punished for arriving forty-five minutes late.

May 1973: Piqued by the comment of a male colleague that she "couldn't organize a piss-up in a brewery," Nadine Smith of the Borough of Hounslow, London, announced that she would prove her skills by hosting a giant party at a nearby brewery the very next week, to celebrate her birthday. Food, drink, a catering service and a band were laid on. The only hitch was that the guests showed up a day early because she posted the wrong date on the employee notice board.

shifts of wit

No question about Muhammad Ali's reputation as "The Greatest." But on the downside, the mighty always have farther to fall. Shortly after defeating Sonny Liston for the heavyweight title, Ali boarded a Pan Am flight for London. Minutes before takeoff, a flight attendant reminded him to fasten his seat belt.

"Superman don't need no seat belt," said Ali.

"Superman don't need no airplane, either," she retorted.

Ali did up his belt.

John Montagu (1718–92) is best known for unintentionally donating part of his title, Fourth Earl of Sandwich, to the lunch-meat industry. Equally unintentional was this opening he gave to John Wilkes, Lord Mayor of London:

"You, Wilkes, will either die on the gallows, or from syphillis!"

To which the mayor replied, "That depends, M'Lord, on whether I embrace your principles or your mistress."

It would have been almost impossible for Frank Case, manager of New York's Algonquin Hotel in the 1920s, not to have assimilated some of the wit of regular patrons such as Robert Benchley and Alexander Wollcott. Proof may be in Case's comment to William Faulkner, whose gloomy work he hated. Faulkner came in one day, complaining of an upset stomach.

"Something you wrote, no doubt," Case suggested.

French monk Abbé Arthur Mugnier (1853–1944), often called the chaplain to Parisian society, was much admired for his grace and charm without ever compromising his integrity as a man of the cloth. Although he is best known among collectors of wit for his reply when asked if he believed in Hell: "Yes, because it is a dogma of the church — but I don't believe anyone is in it." The Abbé showed a human side, too, if the opportunity presented itself. A vain and very plump actress once told him she often gazed at her naked body in the mirror and wondered if that was a sin. "No, madame," Mugnier replied, "defective judgment."

When it comes to George Bernard Shaw ripostes — either giving or receiving — it's a take-your-pick treasure trove. This is my favorite.

American actress Cornelia Otis Skinner played the title role in a revival of Shaw's *Candida*. A series of cables after opening night went like this:

Shaw (to Skinner): "Excellent. Greatest!"
Skinner (to Shaw): "Undeserving such praise."
Shaw: "I meant the play."
Skinner: "So did I."

trivia test

What Doctors Must Do

True Story: The horn on the tiny sports car was so insistent that July evening in London's Regent's Park that Doctor Brian Richards went back to investigate. He had already seen the couple busily engaged in the back seat and had no wish to interfere. After all, this was 1976, and if they were consenting adults, it was no business of his. But the horn indicated trouble. Real trouble, as it turned out, and somewhat beyond Dr. Richards' skills. When he peered, more than a bit embarrassed, into the back window of the tiny green MG, he found a couple locked — as in really locked — in an embrace that required surgery. To the car. The fire department had to cut away the roof, and a small crane was needed to lift the couple out. Under Richards' direction, they were gently separated, and the gentleman was taken away to an orthopedic surgeon. As the ambulance was leaving, the lady asked Dr. Richards if he had any idea what she might tell her husband about the unscheduled modifications to his car!

1.   What doctor's name is associated with
     a) children's stories?
     b) the first Bond movie?
     c) blues guitar?
     d) tooth powder?
     e) the OK Corral?
     f) a bargain with the devil?

2.   Who played Dr. Dolittle in the 1967 movie of that name? Who played the role in a remake in 1996?

3.   What doctor ran the world's first four-minute mile at Oxford, England, in 1954?

4.   Sherlock Holmes always addressed his hero-worshipping colleague formally, or by surname, but Doctor Watson had a first name. What was it?

5.   Far less formal than Sherlock Holmes was the doctor who (according to David Seville) sang, "Oo-ee, oo-ah-ah, ting, tang, walla-walla-bing-bang." Who was he?

6. What distinguishing prop does "Doc," of Walt Disney's Seven Dwarfs, wear? (He's the only one of the seven who does.)

7. What did Doctor Christian Barnard do in 1967 to gain world recognition?

8. Who is Boris Pasternak's doctor?

9. What is trumpeter-bandleader Doc Severinson's first name?

10. To whom did Bugs Bunny say, "What's up, Doc?" most often?

Answers on page 30

this could take a minute, so be sure there's no one waiting

Flush!... And Be a Part of History

First of all, Thomas Crapper is *not* the founding father of the flush toilet. Crapper was a sanitary engineer in England and founded a plumbing fixture company in 1861. He made a few modest improvements to the mechanics of the flush system, but he was very much a marketer, noted for slogans such as "Easy Pull for Easy Flush," and for stamping his name on toilet seats. (The latter practice, allegedly, is what established his name with American soldiers stationed in Britain during World War I; they brought it home as a slang phrase.) Crapper was gone and long forgotten (he died in 1910) until British writer Wallace Reyburn published *Flushed with Pride: The Story of Thomas Crapper* in 1969, and this is what raised his profile so dramatically. Nothing wrong with that, except that the same writer, in 1971, published *Bust-Up: The Uplifting Tale of Otto Titzling and the Development of the Bra,* and anybody who reads that one and believes it, is clearly in trouble. The problem is: after the Titzling venture, it is not unreasonable to assume that Rayburn's Crapper bio may also be, well, crap!

While he may have made his mark in the bathroom, Crapper is definitely not the Alexander Graham Bell of the thunderbox. To begin with, he was too late by a good three thousand years. That's how long ago Minoan nobility on the island of Crete were pulling the handle on overhead tanks. Well east of there, archaeologists have found other bathroom plumbing. In the Indus River Valley of Pakistan, there are sophisticated systems that date from about 3000 B.C. The Egyptians also had working toilets, long before the time of Cleopatra, with copper piping no less, and hot and cold running water. As you might expect, it was the nobility who did most of the flushing — and the bathing. (The nobility got all the hot water. Egyptians priests were required to take four baths a day. But in cold water!)

By Julius Caesar's time, Roman culture had turned the bathroom into a community center. Huge spas dotted the Empire, all of them emphasizing cleanliness and hygiene. Many were open to both men and women. In these spas, small tubs were available for a private soak, or large communal ones for patrons who wanted to chat or carry on business. The same principles applied to the potties. You could sit alone in a cubicle and read (although scrolls must have been a lot harder to manage than bound books like the one in your hand), or, at the Baths of Caracalla for example, choose from over two hundred seats, side by side. More than one commentator of the day observed that the Roman Senate may have been where official debates occurred, but it was in the baths where the real business was done.

With the collapse of the Empire, bathroom history flowed along two separate lines. Much of the social side continued, but the accoutrements — flush toilets, bathtubs, spas, hot and cold running water — disappeared altogether, along with most of the other technical advances of the previous six centuries. And "disappeared" is the operative word, too. Case in point: the great palace built at Versailles in the 1600s. This awesome complex accommodated the French royal family, in addition to a thousand nobles and four thousand servants, but there was no plumbing at all for toilets or bathing. This, despite a huge and complicated water system for the many cascading fountains on the grounds.

What replaced flushing toilets was the chamber pot, along with, it seems, whatever spot in the house that both convenience and urge happened to dictate. Note this public warning, posted in Windsor castle by the chief steward in 1590: *"Let no one, whoever he may be, before, at, or after meals, early or late, foul the staircases, corridors or closets with urine or other filth."* (On the plus side, with habits like these, there must have been very few lineups!) Even if

the chamber pot was put to faithful and diligent use, there was no guarantee of protection from close encounters of the unsanitary kind, for householders tended to empty them into the street each morning, often from a second-floor window.

As for bathing, not only the facilities but the practice itself, disappeared even more quickly than toilets. Christian prudery regarding exposure of the body combined with medieval superstition about washing to usher in 1,500 years of phenomenal body odor. Right through to the early nineteenth century, letters and diaries suggest what it must have been like. "I had my maidservant scrape me today," wrote one English lady in 1720. Another, from France, wrote her sister to describe the new perfume she had acquired from Venice, an ideal concoction apparently, because it pleased her own nose by masking odors she did not like but was "not so strong as to displease Charles, who prefers the strong musk of a horse."

A creative aspect of medieval sanitation, at least in castles, was found in the *garderobe* (wardrobe). In larger, more architecturally designed fortresses, the main bedchambers usually boasted an ensuite. Some of these jutted out over the moat, the straight downward drop thus bypassing a need for plumbing, or at least for drainpipes. Most, however, resorted to the simple chamber pot, which is why the little side room acquired its name, for it was not only a privy but an ideal place to hang clothes. The odors in a typical *garderobe*, it seems, were strong enough to kill body lice, and if the average medieval lord or lady had to choose between stinking a bit or enduring these little creatures, well...

Interestingly, the other legacy of Roman bathroom practice, the social aspect, did not disappear with the same finality as the plumbing did, a fact we can deduce from the number of royal events recorded as taking place in the loo. Charles V, king of Spain, was born in one in 1500. George II of England died in his, in 1760. A few centuries earlier, Henry IV of England survived an assassination attempt in the bathroom because he always took guests along for his morning visit. That practice was double-edged, however. Around the same time (1437), James I of Scotland was murdered by his potty partners. So was Henry III of France in 1589.

Socializing, however, was not universally endorsed. *The Gallant Ethic*, written around 1700, advised young men that if they wished to climb the social ladder, they must learn habits like this: *"If you pass a person who is relieving himself, you should act as if you have not seen him."* No less a worthy than the scholarly Erasmus gave the same advice in 1530: *"It is impolite to greet someone who is urinating or defecating."* (In the same treatise, Erasmus offered his famous advice to always cover the

11

ken
WEBER

sound of a fart by coughing, a remarkably earthbound piece of advice from a theologian.)

Whether Erasmus knew it or not, at the time he was becoming famous, an English nobleman named John Harrington (*not* the origin of "john"; that term comes from "jakes," its early slang equivalent) was inventing — actually reinventing — the flush toilet, and had one installed for Queen Elizabeth in 1596. It was a quite sophisticated model that worked very much like our modern ones, and it might have changed the history of the loo, except that John, Elizabeth's godson, was one of those guys who could not stay out of trouble. He was banished by the queen for publishing racy Italian fiction, and after being forgiven, did it again! The flusher he invented was too closely associated with his scandalous reputation and never caught on.

Therefore, it was not until 1775 that the toilet came back to stay. British watchmaker and mathematician Alexander Cumming devised the system we use today. It was very similar to Harrington's, with one major additional feature: the "S" trap, which fills with water after a flush and prevents odor from seeping back up. Since Cumming, it's all been a matter of fine tuning (including achievements by Crapper, who tinkered with the valve system and is believed to be the first to come up with specially designed seats.)

Curiously, despite the excellence of Cumming's design, and despite a growing awareness of the connection between sewage and diseases such as cholera, flush toilets — like bathtubs and bathing — were slow to catch on (or, perhaps, recatch on). In 1852, for example, two prominent citizens of London, Samuel Peto (builder of Nelson's column in Trafalgar Square) and Henry Cole (father of the Christmas card), put up the cash to install a set of flushable public toilets. Despite heavy advertising, they were soon closed due to lack of use.

Unfortunately for supporters of historical accuracy, Cumming is not the kind of name that lingers in the mind the way Crapper does, despite the imbalance in their relative contributions to the progress of the flush toilet. On the other hand, even an especially melodious name does not help us remember Hilton Martin of Florida either, although he definitely deserves a place of merit in the story of the john. In 1985, Martin cleaned his bathroom bowl with Comet cleanser, hung a Sani-Flush dispenser inside, closed the lid and, fortuitously, left the bathroom and went outside. The combination of sodium hypochlorite and sodium bisulfate in a confined space at just the right temperature wrote a whole new chapter in the lore of the loo. Martin's toilet blew up.

emerge informed

Talk about horsing around. The white horse that Scarlett O'Hara's father rode in *Gone with the Wind* (1939) was also ridden by Lucille Ball in the carousel scene of *Zeigfeld Follies* in 1946. In both movies this proud stallion was a no-name. Lasting fame — and a name — arrived a few years later when he starting toting about a masked rider who called him Silver.

There are only two English words that contain the vowels *a,e,i,o,u,* in that order: *abstemious* and *facetious.* Going the other way, there is only one word: *subcontinental.*

The average life expectancy of humans in the western hemisphere caught up with and passed that of goldfish in 1920. Expectancy for humans at the end of World War I was 48.4 years, while goldfish was 50.1. Since 1920, though, the longevity of humans has continued to increase, while that of goldfish, possibly because of pollution or global warming, has slipped just a bit.

Harshest ever post-mortem job evaluation: The body of Pope Formosus (891–896) was exhumed several weeks after his death and tried for various offences. The event is known in papal history as "The Cadaver Synod." (Formosus was found guilty, and a number of gruesome alterations were made to his body before reinterment.)

The rounded tip on a billiard cue is standard today, thanks to French army captain J. Mingaud. Imprisoned in Paris during the Reign of Terror, he had enough pull to be able to enjoy billiards while inside, and found he was pretty good at it. What was going on outside the walls in Paris may have influenced his next major request, because when his sentence was up he asked to stay in jail for a while to work on his banks and caroms. With the rounded tip he developed, he practiced long and hard and eventually left jail to become the hottest pool shark in Europe.

shifts of (unintended) wit

The *Times* of London, reporting on Queen Victoria's opening of the Clifton Suspension Bridge in 1882

> "After cutting the ribbon, Her Majesty then pissed over the bridge."

The *Toronto Telegram*

> "The mayor agreed that the anus of responsibility rested with him."

The Harrowgate (UK) *Advertiser*

> Yorkshireman Takes the Supreme Pig Title

The *Sowetan* (South Africa)

> Miners Refuse to Work After Death

The *Bulletin* (Antwerp, Belgium) in English

> Lost donkey, answers to the name of Harold. Very attractive, dearly beloved by owner. Last seen in a nun's outfit.

The *Newbury* (UK) *Weekly News*

> Literary Society Hears About Books

The *Oshawa* (Ontario) *Times*

> Wedding gown. Worn once by mistake. Size 9–10. Asking $20

The New Canaan (Connecticut) *Advertiser*

> Our paper carried the notice last week that Mr. Herman Jones was a defective on the police force. This was a typographical error. Mr. Jones is, of course, a detective on the police farce.

The *Nation* (Barbados)

> After a Rastafarian had run amok and amputated one of his mother's and both of his father's hands, a police source described their condition as serious. "They will just have to keep their fingers crossed," he said.

The *Business Day* (South Africa)

> Big Drop in Rainfall

The *Calgary* (Alberta) *Herald*

> A third grain elevator fire in east-central Alberta has investigators wondering if there's a cereal arsonist at work.

hands-free
word adventure

How well do you know your roses?

A rose is a rose in French, Danish and Norwegian, as well as in English. It's *rosa* in Italian, Spanish and Portugese; *ros* in Swedish, *roos* in Dutch, *roja* in Russian, and *roza* in Polish. In German, it's rosen; in Hungarian, rocza; and in Greek and Bohemian, respectively, it's *rhoden* and *ruze*.

Confining yourself to English (although you can try this in Greek or Bohemian, too, if you wish), identify the following sixteen "roses." An annual New Year's Day football game, for example, is the Rose Bowl. A particular kind of stained-glass display in a cathedral is a *rose window*. Et cetera.

1. Guildenstern's buddy

2. A minty spice

3. Cincinnati Red (aka "Mr. Hustle")

4. Couldn't be working out better

5. As opposed to verse...

6. Theatrical producer

7. Robbie Burns' love

8. Child's game

9. Famous archeological find

10. The easy, pleasant route

11. To be collected when opportune

12. Julius and Ethel

13. She's "used" in this song

14. On the Q.T.

15. Started around 1455; ended 1485

16. Biblical plant

Answers on page 30

ken
WEBER

pen-free puzzle posers
(EASY)

1. Noel Hudson was born at 11:58 P.M. on January 18, 1921, just ninety seconds after his sister, Noelle Hudson. Both Noel and Noelle have the same birth parents. Their father was Norman Hudson, and their mother was Nancy Hudson (the former Nancy Erin), who married on June 29, 1917, and had their first child, Nestor Hudson, on March 16, 1919. When Nestor began attending school in 1925, he delighted in explaining to his friends that he had a brother Noel and a sister Noelle, who were *not* twins. *Under what condition could Nestor be correct?*

2. The east to west *Orient Express* left Istanbul at 8 A.M. on Wednesday, July 10, 1884. Because the chief engineer had found serious problems with the primary drive piston on Engine No. 243, the train would be pulled on this trip by only one engine (No. 529) instead of the customary pair. Thus it was not until they were an hour out of Istanbul that the train was able to reach what would be its average speed for this particular run to Paris, 30 kph.

At precisely the same moment, on the same day, the eastbound Orient Express left Paris for Istanbul. There were no problems with the eastbound equipment and the engineer got up to the planned average speed of 60 kph when the train was only twenty minutes past the outskirts of Paris. Under normal conditions, even though Vienna is closer to Istanbul than Paris, the two trains always met there within a few minutes of each other, to exchange mail, diplomatic dispatches and a few high-ticket freight items. Because of the problem on the westbound run this time, it was decided they would stop and make the exchanges at whatever point on the line between Paris and Istanbul that they happened to meet. *On this run, which train will be closer to Vienna when they meet?*

3. Sally had expected to be moved by her visit to the graveyard in Salisbury, for the earliest gravestones dated back to the fifteenth century. What she did not expect, and what bemused her more than a little was the amount of detail and commentary on some of the grave markers. The script carefully chiselled into the monument over the graves of Jonathan and Eva Sacks was particularly touching. The top half said:

HERE LIES THE BELOVED JONATHAN SACKS,
WHO, ON 29 FEBRUARY 1796, LEFT THIS
MORTAL COIL BEHIND, DEAD OF THE
FEVER, AGED BUT 41.

Below this, worked by a different hand was the even sadder account of Eva:

AND HIS WIDOW, EVA, WITH BABE IN ARMS,
WHO DIED IN CHILDBIRTH ON HER VERY
OWN BIRTHDAY, 30 MAY 1794.

Not until she sat down in a pub an hour later did Sally realize what was wrong.

Answers on page 30

going out in style ...more or less

"Bugger Bognor." Unfortunately, this well-known deathbed *mot* is probably apocryphal. According to the story, George V said it when a doctor tried to cheer him with assurances he'd soon be off to the seaside at Bognor Regis. What several bedside attendants have sworn to is that his final words were, "Gentlemen, I am sorry for keeping you waiting like this. I am unable to concentrate." (Which reinforces the story that George's departure was medically accelerated so that the world could be told the next morning in the august *Times*, and not in the tacky afternoon tabloids.)

Among the more crossed-up departure plans is that of William Pitt, the Younger, in 1806. After delivering a suspiciously well-rehearsed line, "My country! Oh, my country!" Pitt maintained silence until he slipped into a coma, but then came out of it again just before he died, to say, "I think I could eat one of Bellamy's meat pies."

What Pitt would surely have appreciated was a final line from Charlotte Whitton, Canada's first woman mayor of a large city. "Do you know what I was?" the feisty Whitton said on her deathbed in 1975. "I was 'hell on wheels'" (a description of her by *Time* magazine that she apparently appreciated).

For departing with class, Spanish dictator Francisco Franco owns a genre standard. When an aide approached his deathbed in 1975 to tell him General García wanted to come in and say goodbye, Franco asked, "Why? Is García going on a trip?"

Franco's line is outclassed not once but twice by Frederick William of Prussia (1795–1861), whose deathbed pastor must have doubled as a straight man. When the pastor told Frederick he must forgive all his enemies, especially his brother-in-law (George II of England), the king told his wife to "Write your brother and tell him I forgive him. But not till after I'm dead."

The same pastor is the one who read Frederick the lines from the Book of Job that say, "Naked came I... and naked shall I return...." To which Frederick responded with his very last breath, "No, not quite naked. I shall have my uniform on."

No political leader, however, has ever outdone Duke Armand de Biron, who was guillotined in Paris in 1793, during the Reign of Terror. "I beg a thousand pardons, my friend," he said to the executioner who had come to take him away, "but permit me to finish this last dozen of oysters."

trivia test

Everyone's Best Friends

The first image seen on TV, in 1930, was a cartoon character, Felix the Cat, but Felix has never achieved the high profile of Sylvester, one of his later colleagues. On the other hand, neither has "Bill." He was the dog in the 1946 movie *The Courage of Lassie*. Almost no one remembers Blue Boy either. He was the hog Will Rogers and Janet Gaynor took to the state fair in 1933, twelve years before one of his progeny went there with Rogers and Hammerstein.

1. What is the name of the spider that rescued a pig named Wilbur?

2. Bambi's two best friends were a rabbit named Thumper and a young skunk whose name was ?

3. What was the name of Dick and Jane's dog (in the primary grade readers)?

4. "Ding dong bell..." Who put pussy in the well?

5. A lion whose "stable name" was Freddy the Freeloader played an important role in the 60s TV series *Daktari* as a cross-eyed lion. His name in the series?

6. Name the lawyer played by Gregory Peck in *To Kill a Mockingbird*.

7. What kind of bird was "The Ugly Duckling"?

8. The first name of a durable (and very competent) NHL goalie for the Toronto Maple Leafs was Walter, but he was better known by a shortened bird name.

9. The last Disney film made while Walt was still alive featured an animated tiger named Shere Khan (voice of George Sanders). What was the movie?

10. What are baby beavers called?

11. Who ate Chicken Little? Turkey Lurkey, too?

12. Who was the H.M.S. *Beagle's* most important passenger?

13. Which of these cats are found in Africa: tiger, jaguar, cougar, ocelot?

14. What birds are in Van Gogh's last painting: *Wheatfield and* _____?

Answers on page 30

ken
WEBER

emerge informed

In all likelihood, there really was a Jack and Jill. It's equally likely they went up the hill, too, for Jack and Jill are believed to have been lovers-on-the-sly, and that's where lovers met in the Somerset village of Kilmersdon in the late fifteenth century. The well is still there on the hill; so is the path where Jack came tumbling down, with Jill tumbling after. The historical account, however, has it that Jack was killed by a falling rock and that Jill died in childbirth.

Alectryomancy is the art of prediction by rooster. The bird is put in the center of a circle of corn, with each kernel representing a letter of the alphabet, and encouraged to peck away. Operating on the same principle as the ouija board, this type of prophecy was popular in ancient Rome.

Irving Berlin could only play in one key, F#. Thus most of his 1,500 songs were composed using only the black keys. Sergei Prokofiev, only three years younger than Berlin, and like Berlin, born in Russia, composed his first opera at age seven, using only the white keys.

The sport(?) of roller derby actually began as a marathon relay race at the Chicago Coliseum in 1935. Twenty-five two-person roller-skating teams met to race a distance equal to that between New York and Los Angeles, and as they went round the oval, first bored, then competitive, promoters were quick to note the crowd's reaction to elbow smashes and other diversions. The evolution of roller derby is not hard to figure out from there.

The ancient Egyptians used a donkey symbol to represent an ignorant person. For the Romans, running into a donkey with your chariot was considered very bad luck. Students of Greek philosopher Chrysippus (c. 265 B.C.) report that he died of laughter at the sight of a donkey eating figs. If all this makes you want to keep donkeys at bay, it may help to know they are allergic to buttercups.

awaiting your solution

The Surprises Pile Up

The day, quite simply, was turning into one surprise after another for Graham Campbell. In the first place, he was a police captain and police *captains* don't run cases. Not on his force anyway. Captains stay in the office and run the lieutenants and the detective sergeants. They run the cases. But two of his guys had phoned in sick this morning — funny how illness attacks people the week before Christmas — so here he was, far from the in-box that was overflowing onto his desk, and instead, conducting an interview in the grand home of the almost-lately-departed Weston Lord. Well, not quite. He'd barely asked his first question of Elayne Lord about her husband's attempted suicide when she sidetracked the process to make tea. Hadn't asked, either, if Graham wanted any. Annoying. Could be worse, though. He could be in the ICU at City Hospital, like Weston.

Graham suddenly realized he'd almost spoken his thoughts out loud. Good thing he caught himself for he wasn't alone. That was owing to another surprise. Just as he'd pressed the button to ring the door chimes at the Lord mansion, Ms Chanel Lajure had scooted up the circular drive and parked behind his car. Not too surprising, really, if you thought about it. Chanel Lajure was Weston's secretary. But she was the very next on his list to be questioned!

And then — this one really took Graham aback — not only did Elayne herself answer the door — he'd expected a maid or something; the sheer size of the house suggested it — but she didn't recognize Lajure! At least, not right away.

"Please, do come in," she'd said to Graham. Very graciously. Everything about her was gracious. A class act, this lady. But her reaction to Chanel Lajure seemed odd.

"I'm sorry, Miss... Who...? Oh goodness! Forgive me! You're Ms Lajure, aren't you? We met at the hospital yesterday, didn't we? That was such a dreadful time. Please come in."

On the way down the hall to the library, Graham learned that Chanel Lajure had been an employee of Weston Lord for only about a week when the suicide attempt had occurred. Well, that was one surprise dealt with, but he still wondered where the servants were. Why Elayne answered the door. And why it was she making the tea. It didn't figure.

The answer came from Elayne herself, who turned out to be as candid as she was gracious.

"I suppose you're aware of Weston's difficulties lately," she said as she came through the French doors with an understated but elegant tea service. Limoges, Graham could see. Pricey. No surprise there. "He lost a great deal in Sri Lanka," she continued. "'Bet on the wrong side.' That's how he put it." She poured milk, then tea into the cup she'd put in front of Chanel Lajure. "I'm sure you know about the political troubles there. A civil war, really. The Tamil people and the Singhalese? All but one of the plantations Weston had contracted with failed to produce their quotas. Some of them not a leaf."

She lifted the lid of the teapot and peered in with a knowledgeable eye. "And that was just the tea. Then the frosts in Columbia turned the coffee market into a shambles. Milk or lemon, Captain…it's Campbell, right? Do you know there has never been a frost of that magnitude so close to the equator?"

"Mi…er…milk. Er…please." Graham didn't drink tea and really wasn't sure what he wanted in it.

"Then with all the pressure for product from his clients, I guess poor Weston just caved in." She took her eyes off the tea things and looked Graham in the eye for the first time. "Of all times…two days before Christmas!"

The intrusive ring of the telephone made all three of them start. Graham noticed Chanel Lajure's hand shake as she put her teacup into the saucer. Elayne's hand shook too. Beneath the carefully applied make-up, her face had paled. "It's the hospital, " she whispered. "I called first thing this morning and they said they would inform me of any change."

"Allow me." Graham said after the fourth ring. "I'll answer it."

Elayne nodded to him and made a simple prayer-like gesture with her hands as Graham made his way to an antique-style rotary telephone at the opposite end of the library.

"My office." He gave the two women a brief, reassuring smile and then turned his back. "No, not at all," Graham said into the mouthpiece. "This case is anything but cut and dried. I've had just one surprise too many this morning."

What is the "one surprise too many" that has apparently made Captain Graham Campbell believe this case is "anything but cut and dried"?

Solution on page 30

for deposit in your "one-up" account

Once-in-a-Lifetime Inserts

That's about how often an opportunity arises naturally to use these. Of course, you can always make your own opportunity by manipulating the conversation.

aposiopesis

(a-POZ-ee-oh-PEE-sis) the act of lapsing into complete silence in the middle of a story. (Although this is actually a rhetorical device, it occurs more frequently as *neuro-ellipsis,* the kind of brain cramp most of your acquaintances experience when they are in the middle of telling a joke.)

lethologica

(leth-oh-LOJ-i-kah) an inability to recall the right word, usually the most important word in the discourse you are currently screwing up as a consequence. (Companion word is *lethonomia:* the same as lethologica but applies to peoples' names.)

glabrous

(GLA-brus) smooth, as in a surface free of hair or other projections. Used frequently in moments of intimacy as in, "Ooh, glabrous!"

lexiphanic

(lex-I-FA-nic) given to pretentious vocabulary, for example, words such as lexiphanic.

merkin

(MUR-k'n) A pubic wig for women. Cited in *Grose's Dictionary of the Vulgar Tongue* as "counterfeit hair for women's privy parts."

napiform

(NA-pi-form) having the shape of a turnip. A word with significant contumelious potential in its adjectival form; for example, "Bernard strode away, unwittingly offering those left behind an unimpeded view of his napaformic bottom."

tremellose

(trem-e-LOHS) having the capacity to shake and quiver excessively, for example, "Wow, Martha! Your lactifera are tremellose!" Which is what you might say if you are playing first base and Martha is running toward you in a uniform she has borrowed from her less well-developed sister.

uliginous

(yu-LI-ji-nus) that which grows in muddy, slimy, swamp-like places. Generally used in early childhood education courses: "It is quite usual for boys especially, to pass through a uliginous phase, most notably if they share a room with a brother of approximately the same age."

uropygium

(eur-o-PI-gee-um) the fleshy, bony protuberance over a fowl's posterior, generally forgotten 364 days of the year but an object of carefully feigned inattention at Thanksgiving dinner, especially during the carving. Often registered in more impoverished vocabularies under "pope's" or "parson's" nose.

shifts of wit

The provenance of this one is unclear, but Winston Churchill usually gets the credit. It was his reaction when a member of his Conservative party crossed the floor: "This, gentlemen, is the first time I have ever seen a rat swimming toward a sinking ship."

Credit for all that follow, however, is clearly established.

Clare Booth Luce: "Whenever a Republican leaves one side of the aisle and goes to the other, it raises the intelligence quotient of both parties."

Thomas Babington Macauley: "The more I read Socrates, the less I wonder why they poisoned him."

Gerald Tyrwhitt-Wilson, 14th Baron Berners, listening to an indignant dissertation by an upper-class British couple about their problems getting seated in a restaurant:

Wife of the couple: "Finally, we had to tell him who we were!"

Lord Gerald: "And who were you?"

Marie Guimard was a popular star of the Paris Opéra during the reign of Louis XVI, although by all reports her dancing style was very static. Her fame, it seems, rested on a combination of artful arm movements and even more artful movement under selected producers. In 1770, Mlle Guimard's arm was broken by falling scenery, an event that elicited this observation from a colleague:

"A pity it isn't her leg; then it wouldn't interfere with her dancing."

George S. Kaufman, who co-wrote *Of Thee I Sing*, disapproved of the way William Gaxton was playing the role at the premiere and sent him a telegram at intermission: "Am sitting in the last row. Wish you were here."

During Pierre Elliott Trudeau's lengthy tenure as Prime Minister of Canada, anonymous donors installed a swimming pool in his official residence. When opposition members made a righteous hue and cry, Trudeau suggested, "You may come over at any time to practice your diving. Even before the water is in."

Irving Layton: "In Pierre Elliott Trudeau Canada has at last produced a political leader worthy of assassination."

hands-free
word adventure

It's *not* funny! But then again...maybe it is!

If you tell people you are fond of puns, they'll likely cringe. It's safer to identify yourself as a *paranomasiphile*. They're more likely to be impressed. They'll be even more impressed when you are the first to complete the following exercise correctly.

   Match each word below with its appropriate paranomasic explanation.

allege	deduce	laundress	moth	rampage
buckboard	filmdom	locate	overbear	tenure
condescend	geometry	macaw	paradox	washable

- gets over the prison wall with a rope

- a really lousy movie

- what lumber used to cost

- what I parked in Boston

- de wild card in dis game

- where hikers stop to have a rest

- in chapter two of the *Shepherd's Gazette*

- attire for summer afternoons

- what the acorn said years later

- what you get after nineure

- two mallards in Saskatchewan

- where it's better to be than under

- done at the ranch once a year, with great care

- green thtuff

- how you greet Catherine at breakfast if you have a hangover

Answers on page 31

pen-free puzzle posers

(MODERATE)

1. When John Denison stepped off the train in Moose Jaw, he was completely taken aback to hear his name called. Hesitantly, almost reluctantly, he turned to look. No one he knew lived in Moose Jaw. Yet, although it took him a minute, he recognized a familiar face coming toward him on the platform. Thinner than he remembered. Certainly older — but aren't we all, he thought.

"Must have gotten married, too," John mumbled to himself, noting the little girl struggling to keep up to his old friend. "Didn't know anything about that!"

"John!" His name was shouted even though the two were close now, and the train noises had subsided. "I can't believe this! The last person I expected to see in Moose Jaw! I guess the world is smaller than we think! Whatever are — oh, sorry, honey. Here, say hello to Mr. Denison."

"Hello, Mifter Denifon," the little girl lisped through missing teeth.

"How nice to meet you," John smiled at her. "What's your name?"

"Fame av my mother," she replied.

"Ah! Then you must be Cindy."

How did John Denison know that?

2. If you were to complete the letter sequence below, where would you place the missing letters I, J, and K respectively: above or below the line?

A   E F H   L M N   T V W X Y Z

B C D   G   O P Q R S U

3. The mental math involved here is pretty simple, after you have figured out the first part…

Imagine the clock face on the front of Big Ben in London. (Big Ben is not the clock; it's the bell behind the clock.) Between 6 A.M. and 6 P.M., how many times will the hands of the clock point in the same direction over the course of one week?

Answers on page 31

27

ken
WEBER

trivia test

Getting the Twentieth Century in Order

January 1, 1900, a new dawn. The century had barely begun when a dirigible flew in Germany, radon was discovered, the Davis Cup was launched, Sanka introduced decaffeinated coffee, the electric vacuum cleaner was patented, *Sheherezade* premiered in Paris... A golden age? Maybe. At the same time, Britain and Germany were deep into an arms race, women in western democracies could not vote, some Georgia planters were found to be still using slaves, and the average life expectancy, planet-wide was just over forty.

1. Place the following events in correct historical order for each group of three.

    a) Pyrex glass is invented by Corning Glass Works.
       Willem Einthoven develops the electrocardiogram.
       Larson and Keeler invent the lie detector.

    b) The first compact discs are put on the market.
       Prozac is cleared for prescription use.
       The VCR makes its debut.

    c) India and Pakistan celebrate first day of independence.
       Dionne quintuplets born at Corbeil, Ontario.
       Bogart and Bergman star in *Casablanca*.

2. Match the championship with its correct debut year.

The World Cup (football)	1903
Citation wins the Triple Crown	1934
The first Masters PGA event	1948
The first World Series (baseball)	1930

3. Place the following TV events in chronological order.

    Jay Leno replaces Johnny Carson on the *Tonight Show*.
    Roseanne debuts on ABC.
    Millions watch live as *Challenger* spacecraft explodes.
    Seinfeld debuts on NBC.

Answers on page 30

emerge informed

Pac-man first hit video screens in 1980. By the end of the century, according to the *Wall Street Journal*, the game had been played over ten billion times. Only once, however, was a perfect score ever recorded. The highest possible score, by the way, is 3,333,360 points.

The word *posh*, for "upscale," comes from Victorians sailing the England–India route. At Southhampton, the better-heeled passengers were always cabined on the port side for the outbound journey in order to catch the onshore breeze. Hence Port Out, or *p-o*. Leaving India, they reversed their booking to the starboard. Hence Starboard Home, or *s-h*.

Although the prototype for fax machines was first developed at MIT in the 1920s, it was not until 1984 that Federal Express offered a new business service they called "Zap Mail," which gave customers a chance to send facsimiles around the continent via phone lines. It didn't take customers long to figure out that it was cheaper to buy their own equipment.

Mozartian one-upmanship: Whenever you hear a Mozart composition introduced, almost always its title will be accompanied by its Köchel number. (Ludwig Köchel is the musicologist who catalogued and numbered Mozart's huge output.) You can impress those about you by dividing the Köchel number you hear by 25, and adding 10. The result will be Mozart's age when he wrote the piece.

If Mozartiana is not to your liking (see above), you may wish to turn to country singer Conway Twitty (1933–93). He was born Harold Jenkins and in 1952 was invited to spring training camp by the Philadelphia Phillies, but didn't attend because he was drafted into the military.

solution/answers

Solution to "The Surprises Pile Up"

Elayne Lord is unquestionably a sophisticated and very experienced hostess who, while pouring tea, is clearly in her element. Yet she has committed an unpardonable social gaffe by pouring milk, then tea, into Chan el Lajure's cup without first asking her how she would like it served. A hostess with Elayne's skills would do this only if she was well acquainted with a guest and could be certain how that guest "takes" tea. When Elayne answered the door, she appeared not to know Chanel Lajure and then remarked that they'd met at the hospital yesterday. Hardly enough time to figure out the niceties of tea serving. The two women must know each other. To Graham Campbell, that's a surprise worth investigating.

Answers to "What Doctors Must Do"

1. (a) Dr. Seuss (b) Dr. No (c) Doc Watson (d) Dr. Lyons (e) Doc Halliday (f) Doctor Faustus 2. Rex Harrison and then Eddie Murphy 3. Dr. Roger Bannister 4. John 5. The Witch Doctor 6. He wears glasses 7. He completed the first successful heart transplant 8. Doctor Zhivago 9. Carl 10. Elmer Fudd

Answers to "Everyone's Best Friends"

1. Charlotte, in *Charlotte's Web* 2. Flower 3. Spot 4. Tommy Green (Tommy Stout pulled her out.) 5 Clarence 6. Atticus Finch 7. A cygnet, a baby swan 8. Turk 9. *The Jungle Book*, an animated version of Rudyard Kipling's classic. 10. Kits 11. Foxy Loxy 12. Charles Darwin

13. None of them (Tiger is Asia: the others are North and South America.) 14. Crows

Answers to "Getting the Twentieth Century..."

1. (a) electrocardiogram, 1903; Pyrex, 1915; lie detector, 1921] (b) VCR, 1976; compact disc, 1983; Prozac, 1988 (c) Dionnes, 1934; *Casablanca*, 1942; India/ Pakistan, 1947
2. World Cup (1930); Citation (1948); Masters (1934); World Series (1903)
3. *Challenger*, 1986; *Roseanne*, 1988; *Seinfeld*, 1990; Jay Leno, 1992

Answers to "Pen-Free Puzzle Posers (Easy)"

Nestor would be correct if Noel and Noelle are two of a set of triplets. (As they are. He deliberately avoided mentioning Norma, who was born a minute before Noelle.)

When the trains meet, they will be the same distance from Vienna, no matter where they are along the line.

Don't be distracted by the date of February 29, for 1796 was a leap year. What is wrong is that Eva Sacks died nearly two years before Jonathan did, so she could not have been his widow.

Answers to "Hands-Free Word Adventure: How well do you know your roses?"

1. Rosenkrantz 2. Rosemary 3. Pete Rose 4. Coming up roses 5. prose 6. Billy Rose 7. A red, red rose 8. Ring Around the Rosie, a game that originated during the Black Death. "Rosies" were

red bubos that formed in rings around the armpit. After a few hours the victim began sneezing ("Husha!") and usually died ("All fall down.")   9. Rosetta Stone   10. the primrose path   11. Rosebuds   12. Rosenberg   13. Second-hand Rose   14. sub rosa   15. War of the Roses   16. Rose of Sharon

Answers to "Hands-Free Word Adventure: It's *not* funny! But then again...maybe it is!"

allege, where hikers stop to have a rest; *buckboard,* what lumber used to cost; *condescend,* gets over the prison wall with a rope; *deduce,* de wild card in dis game; *filmdom,* a really lousy movie; *geometry,* what the acorn said years later; *laundress,* attire for a summer afternoons; *locate,* how you greet Catherine at breakfast if you have a hangover; *macaw,* what I parked in Boston; *moth,* green thtuff; *overbear,* where it's better to be than under; *paradox,* two mallards in Saskatchewan; *rampage,* in chapter two of the *Shepherd's Gazette*; *tenure,* what you get after nineure; *washable,* done at the ranch once a year, with great care.

Answers to "Pen-Free Puzzle Posers (Moderate)"

John's friend, the one who called to him, was Cindy.

The letters are placed by shape: straight line letters above the line, and curved letters below. Thus I and K go above the line and J below.

The hands of the clock overlap and point in the same direction eleven times between 6 A.M. and 6 P.M. Times seven days is seventy-seven times. (Some people actually need to take a watch or clock and spin the hands around until they accept the correct answer. While they are doing that, you can tell them about the time in May 1945 when so many starlings sat on the minute hand of the Big Ben clock that it lost five minutes!)

section TWO

emerge informed

A record in modern art display was broken in 1999 when a closer look revealed that one panel of Gaetano Previati's triptych *Fall of the Angels* had the blessed spirits going the wrong way. This ethereal traffic violation endured at Rome's National Gallery of Modern Art for 89 days. The previous record holder was Henri Matisse's *Le Bateau,* which sailed upside down for 47 days at the Museum of Modern Art in New York, in 1951. In both cases, the correct view was published in the respective guidebooks — which suggests that, with modern art, either no one pays attention or that it doesn't matter anyway.

The modern version of the mini-skirt first appeared in 1965. Among the official reactions to it were jail sentences (in Egypt, the Congo, Malagasy Republic, even Greece, where men had worn a version of it 2,000 years before); violent readjustments (in Zambia, where male gangs set upon wearers and forcibly lowered the hemlines); and restrictions (in Disneyland, where gate attendants measured the gap from knee to hemline and refused to admit the overexposed).

Rule on this one. Sam Snead and Jimmy Hines were tied at the 13th hole, a par 3, during the 1938 PGA championship. Snead's tee shot had landed inches from the cup. Hines's was in a sandtrap at the edge of the green. Hines's chip shot hit Snead's ball and both balls went into the cup. (Officials awarded both golfers a birdie two.)

The Katzenjammer Kids, with Hans and Fritz, is the world's longest running newspaper comic strip. It first appeared in the *New York Journal* on December 12, 1897.

It's well known that fidelity in the avian world (swans notwithstanding) often takes second place to preservation of the species. No bird takes the latter role more seriously than the female jacana. Although convent school biology classes continue to emphasize the tropical jacana's ability to walk on lily pads, the bird has a far more notable claim to fame, in that the female participates in more copulations per hour than any other bird in the world. DNA studies of the eggs (to add insult, it's the male who sits on the nest) show that 50 to 75 percent of a typical clutch have different fathers!

 ## shifts of wit

Sir Thomas Beecham had just raised the baton for the first notes of a morning rehearsal when he noticed a new face among the woodwinds.

"Mr...?" he inquired.

"Ball," was the reply.

"I beg your pardon?"

"Ball, Sir Thomas."

"Ball? Ah, Ball! Very singular."

When Hollywood director Billy Wilder was "loaned" to Germany after World War II to help re-establish the German film industry, he also took part in bringing back the famed Oberammergau Passion Play. Local German officials, with the support of the U.S. command, wanted the actor who had played Christ before the war to take up that role again, even though the man had been a known supporter of the Nazi party. When Wilder was asked to cast him, he agreed, "as long as we use real nails."

Despite his many years in Paris, artist James Whistler never did manage to get a firm handle on the French language. Not that the deficiency impeded him. When a companion began to order dinner for both of them at a restaurant one night, Whistler huffily grabbed the menu and delivered his own request — in his own French.

"I am perfectly capable," Whistler explained sharply.

"Of course, you are," the companion replied, "but just now I distinctly heard you order a flight of stairs."

On the day he was fired from Columbia Studios, scriptwriter Herman Mankiewicz was part of a small group in the executive dining room enduring a tirade from studio head Harry Cohn, whose opinions, everyone at Columbia knew, often took precedence over common sense. Cohn was explaining how he sat in a projection room and judged a picture as good or bad. "If my fanny squirms," he explained, "it's bad. If my fanny doesn't squirm, it's good. Simple as that."

"Imagine," came Mankiewicz's too audible murmur, "the whole world wired to Harry Cohn's ass."

Sometimes the best shifts of wit are offered in complete innocence. When English essayist Charles Lamb (1775–1834) was only three, but already a precocious reader, he was made to accompany his family on a Sunday afternoon graveyard visit. After reading the number of stones praising the various deceased as "beloved," "loving," "kind," "upright" and so on, he turned to his sister Mary and asked, "Where are all the naughty people buried?"

not their finest hour

You don't have to be a politician to choke yourself with your foot...

"I can't really remember the names of the clubs we went to," replied basketball star Shaquille O'Neal when asked if he had visited the Parthenon during a trip to Greece.

But then if you are a politician, what you have to say is more important...

"I suppose three things certainly come to mind that we want to say thank you. The first would be our family. Your family, my family, which is composed of an immediate family of a wife and three children, a larger family with grandparents and aunts and uncles. We all have our family, which ever that may be."

Former U.S. vice-president Dan Quayle

Some politicians can offer their wisdom in more than one language...

"When you look at the future of agriculture, you realize that food will become very important in the years to come."

> Canadian prime minister Jean Chrétien, who also owns
> the following gem (spoken in French):

"Am I the only one around here with half a brain?"

Not that politicians are without support from the shining stars of academe..

"This man [Prime Minister Chretién] has been before this system and his acuity because of that is the type of thing we are looking for in the leaders we are looking for."

> Colin Campbell, professor, Georgetown University

Seems things are safest when simplicity reigns...

U.S. President Ronald Reagan in May 1985: "How's your crisis going?"

Italian Prime Minister Bettino Craxi: "Pretty well."

 trivia test

Trick or Treat

In the ancient Celtic (and Anglo-Saxon) calendars, the last day of the year was All Hallows. Beginning on All Hallows eve, the ancients believed, spirits of the dead would roam about looking for their former homes. Therefore, many people stayed outside and built huge bonfires so the spirits could see in the dark (and probably so the people themselves could keep warm). Hermits, eccentrics and odd-looking loners, who just might be spirits — no one was prepared to take a chance — knew this was a good time to show up looking for handouts. As time went on, children especially began to dress as spirits and call on neighbors, who would give them treats so that these "spirits" would not do them any harm.

1. Although this particular ghost has never been near Elm Street (that we of know of) he has a friend named "Nightmare." Who is this ghost?

2. It was a bad idea to cross Vlad the Impaler, ruler of Wallachia from 1456 to 1462. By what name do we know Vlad today, thanks to writer Bram Stoker?

3. Nothing scarier than a peeping tom at your window. Legend has it that there really was a peeper named Tom. What famous lady did he peep at?

4. A delightfully non-scary Hallowe'en practice these days is collecting for UNICEF. What do the letters U.N.I.C.E.F. stand for?

5. Alfred Hitchcock's 1960 movie *Psycho* is still the benchmark against which all scary movies are judged. Within two, how many Oscars did *Psycho* win?

6. "Black Cat" Gagnon played hockey (for the Canadiens). Johnny "Big Cat" Mize played baseball (Yankees and Cardinals). What did the "The Hillbilly Cat" play?

7. *The Modern Prometheus* is the subtitle of a novel written by Mary Shelley in 1818. What is the main title of her novel?

8. Oscar the Grouch lives in a garbage can. Where does Oscar Zoraster Phadrig Isaac Norman Henckle Emmanuel Ambroise Diggs live?

9. Very special fears: Triskadecaphobia is fear of the number 13. Selenophobia is fear of the moon. More common than both of these, however is ergasophobia. Fear of what?

Answers on page 58

this could take a minute, so be sure there's no one waiting

What Happened to Mary Twice Nightly

To a movie-going culture used to "Two thumbs up!" or "Awesome! Stupendous!" or "Leaves you hanging on to your seat," learning what happened to Mary two times every night might be more than a little interesting. However, even though that promise was spread across the marquee of the cinema in Haddington, Scotland, for much of 1912, audiences never did find out for sure. They turned out in droves, though — a tribute to the power of publicity, even if it is unintentional. *What Happened to Mary* was a twelve-part serial starring Mary Pickford as a foundling searching for the truth of her past (she finds it in episode twelve). The manager of the Harrington cinema decided to run the same episode before and after the main feature every night. All he lacked was punctuation. Thus, "What Happened to Mary Twice Nightly."

The Harrington sign was a small one — not that it failed to attract attention. Somewhat larger was the blatant appeal of a cinema in Glasgow a few years later, when, also without benefit of a comma or period, foot-high letters announced *GEORGE WASHINGTON SLEPT HERE WITH ANN SHERIDAN.*

Still, both are fairly tame compared to the way Cecil B. DeMille's 1927 epic *King of Kings* was presented to the public in New York. "Dramatic Magnificence!" the advertising declared. And if that weren't enough, a patron would also encounter "Spectacular Splendor, Riotous Joy, Tigerish Rage, Undying Love, Terrifying Tempests," and "Appalling Earthquakes." Not bad for a movie based on the New Testament — and without sound, too!

From the very beginning of cinema history, theater owners simply adapted the publicity styles they had been using to promote carnivals and freak shows, circuses and vaudeville: namely, exaggeration. It was a habit of big-time owners in the cities, and of the tiny, 50-seat parlor managers in little villages. When Sadlers Wells in London introduced its "Theatrograph" in 1896, the public was promised a "mighty mirror of

Promethean Photographs and a superbly brilliant and electrifying entertainment specially adapted to cheer the toiling millions." In 1908, at a village theater a few miles away, the owner, obviously convinced that patrons had forgotten both their history lessons and their calendars, promised "the most extraordinary invention of modern times, as presented before the Emperor Napoleon."

Naturally, as moviegoers became more sophisticated, not to mention cynical, publicity claims had to be toned down somewhat, but the occasional bit of absolutely improbable hype still managed to creep in. A completely gushy romance produced in India in 1982 and entitled *Red Rose* was released with the somewhat pedestrian cutline: "Petals from a beautiful film flower named Red Rose." One publicist blithely inserted two convenient typos. He put a colon after "flower," and then changed "named" to "naked." Another added, "Adapted from *The Yorkshire Ripper.*" Although the industry takes a dim view of such distortions, it has always turned a blind eye to advertising that selects whatever words and phrases it wants from reviews. Thus *Variety's* review of *The American Prisoner* (1929), which began "Save for direction, story, dialogue, acting, and being a period picture, this is a good one," was cited in ads around North America as " *Variety* calls it 'a good one.'"

Today's movie producers make effective use of the preview, or trailer, a come-on publicity style that was first tried in Paris in 1898 but which became an industry all its own in 1920. It is not unusual today, especially for movies aimed at teenage audiences, for producers to put together as many as five different previews of the same flick, each geared toward demographics such as ethnicity and social class.

According to creative director Sol Parker, trailers "should always be better than the movie." Their success has done much to wipe out the wonderful gimmicks of years ago. Gimmicks like the promise by a theater in Georgia to give away, free, a one-piece coat hanger to every patron. (In 1914 that was no small offer.) Those who paid their admission were given a tiny envelope containing a nail.) Another theater (in 1912) promised to give away a baby on opening night, and published a declaration that the baby's mother was entirely willing, and indifferent to the outcome. The same manager — although one doubts his effort was needed — arranged for an intensive letter-to-the-editor campaign, condemning a mother who would do such a thing. While the packed house — including a large contingent of local police — held its collective breath on the big night, the manager gave away a baby pig! Still

other cinemas made arrangements with grocery
stores to include a thirteenth egg with every dozen,
the extra specimen stamped with details of upcom-
ing features.

Giveaway promotions pretty much died out by the time
talkies became popular, though as late as 1986, French video distributors
scraped the bottom of the taste barrel by giving away Ku Klux Klan
masks to promote *Mississippi Burning*. Also pretty much gone are the
marquee publicity stunts popular in the 1930s and 1940s, perhaps
because of Disney Studios' experience in promoting the premiere of
Pinocchio in 1940. The studio hired eleven very short adults to hang
around on top of the marquee on opening day and generally "be funny."
Problem was, by noon they had become entirely bored and tipped the
caterer's deliveryman to pass up several bottles of liquor with their lunch.
By mid-afternoon, about half the group had taken off their clothes and
were dancing around the marquee naked. When they began to pee down
on passersby, the police arrived with ladders and blankets to cart them
away. The premiere was a sellout, but Disney opted for tamer stunts
thereafter.

Of all the methods used to promote movie-going, one of the least
frequently used seems to be complete honesty. Not that it hasn't been
tried. In 1940 a Minnesota theater manager beefed up his showing of
Windjammer with a lottery. "See a lousy show and win $70," he adver-
tised. In Nebraska, a few years later, another manager offered, "Double
Feature: One Good Show and One Stinker." Still another — one who
obviously knew why his patrons go to the cinema — advertised *Fighting
American* (1924) as "guaranteed not to make you think." None of
these, however, approaches the bang-on clarity of a drive-in marquee in
North Carolina in the 1960s. "Two Features" was all the sign ever said.
"Two Features" was the only information he needed to display, the manager pointed out, along with "Open," because "the people who patron-
ize this drive-in don't care what's playing."

At $6,000 a year, Tony "The Count" Mullane was one of major league baseball's highest paid players in the '80s — the *1880s!* He was well paid because he was good. And what made him so good was that he threw right *and* left! Mullane broke in with Detroit in the National League in 1881 and ended with Toronto in the Eastern League in 1899. His best year? Throwing from both sides in 1887, his line was 31 and 17, with six shutouts. What makes that even more spectacular is that 1887 was the season the major leagues experimented with four strikes.

Talk about waiting for your next hit. In 1958 Cuban bandleader Perez "Prez" Prado made his name with a quasi-Latin, quasi-rock-and-roll song, "Patricia," which hung out on the top ten charts for weeks. This, at a time when big songs blew in and out in days. He didn't have another hit for 36 years, and then only in England. The song, "Guaglione," became a British hit in 1994 when Guinness Breweries used it in an ad. Prado had recorded "Guaglione" back in 1958 when he did "Patricia."

Out of the frying pan... Until the 1950s, when antibiotics became readily available, it was still common practice to induce malaria into a patient suffering from tertiary syphilis. The cure rate for the syphilis was respectably high, but the patient then had to deal with malaria. Some choice.

Among the legacies of England's King George IV (intelligent achievement most notably excluded) is the inadvertent creation of a popular brand name. When the Royal Chef presented His Majesty with a piquant steak sauce he'd whipped up, George is reputed to have pronounced it "Absolutely A-1!" George died in 1830 of cirrhosis, gout, nephritis, dropsy and ruptured blood vessels in the stomach, a consequence of being into the sauce for much of his adult life. Not the A-1.

It might be tempting to drink giraffe milk before a big game because it's seven times richer in protein than cow's milk, but not if you're playing a game like basketball. Giraffes cannot distinguish green, yellow and orange, so your passing could be adversely affected. On the other hand, a giraffe cannot sleep lying down for more than about five minutes at a time, so you might want to try the milk in your staff coffee room.

hands-free
word adventure

"I always forget how to spell that."

It follows that a language that ships by truck, ships by rail, and even ships by ship (not to mention one that has feet that smell and noses that run) will also have some interesting spelling challenges.

In the two columns below, there are eight words spelled *correctly*. Which are they?

dessicate	concensus
annisette	license
privilege	accomodate
ukelele	supersede
separate	rhythmn
persuant	removeable
attachment	anticeptic
commiserate	commitee
heterogeneous	prodigous
combustable	optimism

Answers on page 58

wit off the wall

2 P.M., Wed., May 7, Osler Hall
Lecture 4 in the series: "The Unexpected in Obstetrics"
   Mary had a little lamb

What Will You Do When Jesus Comes?
   Move Gretzky Back on Defense

Passengers! Please Do Not Cross the Yellow Lines
   It takes us forever to untangle them again.

Place Coins in Slot
Wait for Coins to Drop
Pull Handle Out All the Way
Package Will Appear Below
   If this is sex it sounds pretty boring.

Bring Your Kids to Disneyworld!
   And leave the little buggers there!

Do Not Touch Unattended Bags
   (But you might try chatting them up.)

Please Do Not Throw Matches Into the Urinals
   The crabs have learned to vault.

Mr. Chan will be cremated on Monday, April 3 at 2 P.M.
   Can you put him on low? I can't make it till 3.

Bill Clinton has no principles!
   Tell him to take a bath. It worked for Archimedes.

Jesus Died for Your Sins!
   There you go, I didn't even know he was sick.

Please Do Not Flush While the Train Is Standing in a Station
   Except in Boise

Faith Can Move Mountains!
   Now that must be one awfully big broad!

pen-free puzzle posers

(EASY)

Limit yourself to thirty seconds or less to get this answer.

1. Add two thousand and twenty to one thousand and twenty.

Add ten to the answer above.
Add ten more.
Now add twenty.
Add ten more.
Now add ten again.

What is your answer?

2. Under Mono Cliff Road, there is a drainage culvert just wide enough for one person to crawl through. The Dufferin County Roads Department acknowledges this culvert is a difficult one to repair because it is so narrow. When an emergency repair was needed after a sudden downpour, the department sent its only two available crewpersons at the time. Both were known to be stout. Despite this apparent disadvantage, the two crawled into the culvert from opposite ends, did what needed to be done, and then each exited at the end opposite to the one he went in. *How did they accomplish this entrance and exit without widening the culvert?*

3. The excellent reputation of the harvest workers at the Rockwood cranberry bog is fully justified by their basket fill rate: one basket per minute. This rate actually outpaces that of Rockwood's mechanical picking equipment (which, under optimum conditions, fills baskets at a rate of one and a half per minute) because the workers have a co-operative system so efficient that the amount in each basket they pick by hand doubles every second. *When is one of their baskets half full?*

Answers on page 57

ken
WEBER

going out in style

Lines from Those Who Were There

"Is the bloody man dead yet?" asked Caitlin Thomas, wife of Dylan, at the time of her husband's demise. The Thomases' marriage was the antithesis of Ward and June Cleaver's. Caitlin once described it as "raw, red, bleeding meat!"

At Windsor castle, one morning in 1821, the groom of the bedchamber was instructed to awaken George IV and tell him Napoleon had died.

"Sire, your bitterest enemy is dead," said the groom as softly as he could into the sleepy royal ears.

"Is she, by God?" was His Majesty's reply.

Unfortunately for George, he had to wait a few more weeks before his hated wife, Queen Caroline, made her departure.

Wits such as Dorothy Parker were major contributors to the reputation of President Calvin Coolidge, known as "Silent Cal." When Parker was told that Coolidge had died, her quip was, "How can they tell?

Although Coolidge was indeed a man of few words, he was not without some verbal dexterity of his own. When a dinner guest told him she'd made a bet that she would get at least three words out of him, he smiled very slowly and said, "You lose."

When the wife of super genius Freiderich Gauss (credited with concepts such as the Bell Curve while still a teenager) lay dying in her bedchamber, Gauss was absorbed with a new problem in his study. The doctor tapped on his door to tell him that the final moment had come.

"Tell her to wait a moment until I'm through," he said without looking up.

The response of Albert Einstein's nurse when asked what his final words were: "I haven't the foggiest idea what he said." Einstein spoke them in German and the nurse spoke only English.

"Well, that kind of puts the damper on even a Yankee win."

The words of Phil Rizzuto during a Yankee game. The network had broken in to announce the death of Pope Paul VI. Rizzuto's comment was made on-air.

"Well, now at least I know where he is."

A remark to Lord Esher by the long-suffering Queen Alexandra after the death of her philandering husband, Edward VII, in 1910.

trivia test

Let There Be Peace

There is much irony in the life of Alfred Nobel, whose fortune created the Nobel Prizes. He thought that by inventing dynamite, he would bring peace to the world, because no country would have the nerve to use something so powerful in war. (Dynamite was introduced early in 1866; in the same year, it was used in bombs for the first time.) The prizes themselves are an irony. In 1888 a Swedish newspaper printed an obituary for Nobel's brother but goofed and turned it into Alfred's obit! In the text they referred to him as a "merchant of death." That is what shocked Alfred into leaving his fortune to humankind.

ken
WEBER

1. Four of these ten Nobel Peace Prize laureates below were elected to the top political office in their respective countries. Which four?

   Ralph Bunche (1950)
   Albert Schweitzer (1952)
   Lester Pearson (1957)
   Dag Hammarskjold (1961)
   Willy Brandt (1971)
   Andrei Sakharov (1975)
   Menachem Begin (1978)
   Lech Walesa (1983)
   Desmond Tutu (1984)
   J. Dalai Lama (1989)

2. The document that ended war with Japan was signed aboard the battleship USS *Missouri*, in 1945. Where did officials gather in 1919, to sign the treaty that ended war with Germany?

3. Of calpac, caltrop and calumet, which one is a "peace pipe"?

4. In what country is the 2,000 km (1,200 mile) Peace River?

5. Mars is the Roman god of war. Who is the Roman goddess of peace?

6. The words "peace on earth and mercy mild" appear in what Christmas carol?

7. "We shall beat our swords into ploughshares…" At what world-famous building will you find this quotation at the main entrance?

8. What's missing in this beatitude: "Blessed are the peacemakers, for they shall be called the _____ of God."

9. The first Nobel Peace Prize (1901) was shared by Frederic Passy and Henri Dunant. The former, unfortunately, is pretty much forgotten. What did Dunant do to deserve the recognition?

Answers on page 58

emerge informed

In 1950, former U.S. Army private George Jorgensen Jr. left New York for Copenhagen. Two years later he returned as Christine Jorgensen. George/Christine had to undergo a whole slew of operations and endure over 2,000 hormone injections to make the change. A sharp contrast with another of Mother Nature's creations, who does the same thing every year — without even going to Denmark. In early spring, a jack-in-the-pulpit bursts out of the ground as a male, but by the time it flowers it's a female.

Debate continues over who is/was the greatest violinist of all time, but there is no debate whatever over who is the fastest. It's Nicolo Paganini (1782–1840). He once performed his "Perpetuela" in 3 minutes, 3.74 seconds. That averages out to just over 12 notes per second. Fellow musicians present during the timing (performance?) followed the score and insist he didn't miss anything, even though conceivably 12 notes per second is faster than the average human can listen. Stopwatches, by the way, were invented in 1776.

The first Super Bowl took place in 1967 in the Los Angeles Coliseum. The Green Bay Packers beat the Kansas City Chiefs 35–10, and there were almost 40,000 empty seats!

Manufacturers of toothpicks prefer white birch.

March 21 is Johann Sebastian Bach's birthday. March 21 is also the day (in 1935) when Iran became Iran again, after being Persia for several hundred years. Bach never visited Iran when it was Persia. March 21 is the official feast day of Saint Serapion of Thmuis and he never went to Iran either.

ken
WEBER

for deposit in your "one-up" account

Some myths for you to puncture

The very bottom tip of the continent of Africa is not the Cape of Good Hope. Cape Agulhas is half a degree of latitude (actually, 29 minutes of latitude) south of Good Hope. So it's Agulhas at the bottom.

$$\$\$$$

Chubby Checker did not originate the twist. That accomplishment belongs to R&B performer Hank Ballard, who wrote and recorded "Twist" in 1959 (lifting the melody from an old R&B song, "What'cha Gonna Do?") Ballard's big chance with it on *The Dick Clark Show* was a bust, but a re-recording of it and a new performance by Chubby in 1961 started a fad. Chubby, by the way, was Ernest Evans, a performer with an amazing talent for imitating other singers, but with a name that aroused zero attention. It was Dick Clark's wife who came up with "Chubby Checkers."

$$\$\$$$

The first episode of *Leave It to Beaver* to be filmed was not the first one to hit the airwaves. In the first episode, the Beav and Wally keep a pet alligator in the toilet tank in the Cleaver's bathroom, but at that time CBS policy did not permit toilets to be shown. (For fans of coincidence: the first episode appeared October 4, 1957, the same day the USSR launched *Sputnik I.*)

$$\$\$$$

Although Joni Mitchell wrote "Woodstock," the hit song about the biggest event in rock-and-roll history, the three day love-in known as "The Woodstock Festival," she was never there. She watched it on TV from New York City. She skipped the festival to be on *The Dick Cavett Show*. The festival actually took place at Bethel, New York, not Woodstock — an appropriate distinction for a culture that readily adopted phrases such as "It's, like, nowhere, man!"

$$\$\$$$

Peter Minuit did not cheat the natives when he bought Manhattan Island for $24 worth of beads and fish hooks in 1626. Rather, it was Peter who got stung. He gave the stuff to the Canarsees people, who were over touring for the day. They lived in what would one day be Brooklyn. Peter should have been dealing with the Weckquaesgeeks. As it turned out, the proper owners lost the island anyway, and never even got the fish hooks!

pen-free puzzle posers
(CHALLENGE)

1. Saneya knew instinctively that it was a test. For one thing, none of the others at the well were jostling her for position on this trip, taking advantage of her tiny size as they usually did so they could have the best spot to lower their containers down to the sweet water below. For another, she'd been told to bring back precisely three quarts, no more, no less. And she'd been given an eight-quart jug with no measuring marks on it. Nor were there any on the seven-quart one that someone had carelessly left beside the path on the way to the well. But Saneya was going to prove something to them this time. She could use these two jugs. If they wanted three quarts, they'd get three. But how?

2. Without turning any of the pages in your copy of *The Toilet Papers* to look, how many times does 6 occur in the page numbering between pages 1 and 100?

3. Vera promised her family she would stop smoking as soon as the pack in her purse was empty. It contained sixteen unsmoked cigarettes. Because they were delighted by her promise, neither her husband nor her children said anything when they noticed her buying a package of cigarette papers. Nor did they say anything each time they saw her roll four butts into a new cigarette. Vera kept her word, however. When all the tobacco was gone, she did indeed quit smoking. How many cigarettes did she smoke between the time of her promise and the time the tobacco was gone?

Answers on page 57

ken
WEBER

hands-free
word adventure

You know more Latin than you realize

Someone whose first language is Hungarian or Pushtu or Dzongkha must find it curious that, in English, one can see stars when they are "out," but can't see lights when they are "out" (unless it's "light out"). Another struggle, but one shared with some English speakers (some, not you), is understanding phrases from Latin that have been adopted *corpus intactum* into English.

Match each used-in-English Latin phrase in column A with its meaning in column B.

A	B
1. quid pro quo	a) afterward
2. ex libris	b) in its place, established
3. caveat emptor	c) there is no arguing about tastes.
4. non compos mentis	d) from the books of
5. sine qua non	e) wonderful to tell
6. post facto	f) tit for tat
7. de gustibus non est disputandum	g) an indispensable condition
8. in situ	h) not of sound mind
9. ipso facto	i) let the buyer beware
10. mirabile dictu	j) the thing (fact, idea, act) by itself

Answers on page 58

trivia test

Gimme That Old-Time Rock-and-Roll

Trivia lovers know that rock-and-roll buffs are fanatics in the same league as *Star Trek* buffs. While Trekkies can tell you that it was three Romulan ships (not four, as so many believe) that surrounded the *Enterprise* in the "Enterprise Incident," fans of rock-and-roll obscura can reach deep to tell you that John Lennon played a harmonica in the Beatles' first three singles. Or that the great Chuck Berry (possibly the real father of rock-and-roll) held a degree in cosmetology from Gibbs Beauty School. They know that Buddy Holly's mother was his co-writer for "Maybe Baby." These are the fans that would turn over their collection of eight-track tapes to charity (or more likely to a garage sale) for the opportunity of hearing the never released "Million Dollar Quartet," an impromptu jam session at Sun Records in 1956 with Johnny Cash, Elvis Presley, Carl Perkins and Jerry Lee Lewis. It was recorded, but never released.

1. What did old time folk and blues singer Muddy Waters give to the Rolling Stones?

2. In the so-called "British invasion" that followed the Beatles in the 1960s, a group called the Yardbirds changed their lead guitarist four times. In rapid succession, there was Tony Topham, Eric P. Clapp, Jeff Beck, then Jimmy Page. Which one, with an adjusted name, was soon bigger than the Yardbirds?

3. The phrase "rock-and-roll" was around long before it was used to describe a style of music. What did it mean to those who used it?

4. What rock-and-roll singer provided the title for the Beatles' hit "Lucy in the Sky with Diamonds" when he was only a child?

5. Who wins the competition for most songs to reach number one on the North American charts: Elvis Presley or the Beatles?

6. In 1975 this "blue-collar singer" appeared simultaneously on the covers of *Time* and *Newsweek*. Who was it?

ken
WEBER

7. Roberta Flack turned "Killing Me Softly With His Song" into a huge hit, but it was written by Lou Lieberman, who was "killed" watching a singer perform "American Pie" in a concert. Who was the "killer"?

8. An American Bandstand rule was that a singer had to mime his record. Only one fiery pianist was never able to do it and had to sing live. Who?

9. By what name is Reginald Dwight very well known?

Answers on page 58

 more wit off the wall

Objects in the Mirror Are Dumber Than They Appear

Sign on the underside of a toilet seat:
Thank God! A Man at Last!

Dyslexia lures!

Back in a minute!
Godot

Abstinence is the thin edge of the pledge.

Brian is a fagot!
At least I can spell fagget

Humpty Dumpty was pushed!

The difference between our head office and a cactus plant is that the plant has its pricks on the outside.

If God really wanted the metric system, Jesus would have had ten apostles.

Donna is just like my piano. When she's not upright, she's grand.

Our Pledge
Local 349 is in a legal strike position, and our employer refuses to negotiate in a fair and reasonable manner. However, we assure travelers we will do our best to ensure your luggage arrives at your destination.
Signed: Wrong-way Corrigan, President, Local 349

Think about it, Superman gets into Clark Kent's pants every morning.

I've changed my mind. To hell with the meek! God

emerge informed

Fictional Chinese detective Charlie Chan of the Honolulu police first appeared in a novel entitled *The House Without a Key,* serialized in the *Saturday Evening Post* in 1925. Over the next several decades Charlie Chan starred in 46 feature movies, a long-running radio show and a TV program, but not once was Charlie played by a Chinese actor. Japanese actors played him twice in the movies; actor Ralph Camargo played him with a Spanish accent on radio. Even Ed Begley had the role for a while. But nobody Chinese.

During the medal awards for heavyweight wrestling at the 1952 Olympics in Helsinki, there was something vaguely familiar about the bronze medal winner from Great Britain. No wonder. For years, movie-goers had watched Ken Richmond hammer the gong at the beginning of J. Arthur Rank movies. His body was then, and still is, one of the most frequently seen male bodies in the world.

Don't try this at home. The longest flight of a popped champagne cork at room temperature is 177 feet 9 inches. This contribution to human achievement was arranged by Heinrich Medicus at the Woodbury Vineyards in New York state, in June 1988.

In the thirteenth century, European intellectuals flocked to the great teacher and Dominican monk Albertus Magnus (real name: Albert, Count von Bollstadt). Scholar, theologian, teacher, chemist (he isolated arsenic) and canonized saint, Albert was nevertheless a man of his time. Among his surviving writings is this recipe for an aphrodisiac: "Take three pubic hairs and three from the left armpit. Burn them in a hot shovel. Pulverize, insert into a piece of bread. Dip in soup and feed to a lover."

People who believe there were roses in the Garden of Eden may see their theory reinforced by a fossilized rose found at Florissant, Colorado, that Smithsonian paleobotanists have pegged at 40 million years old. That's older than the dinosaurs, so roses must have survived them, too. Must be the thorns.

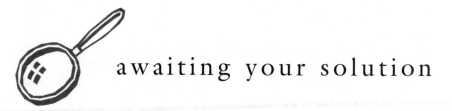

awaiting your solution

Two Shots in the Antique Store

Because he was a rookie, Cam Lindsey was determined not to make a mistake. Also because he was a rookie, he was going by the book. And the book said that the first officer on the scene of any felony — indeed anything that even looked like a felony — must call for the senior detective on duty.

Cam was a beat cop. He'd been on foot patrol for exactly eleven days now, his first assignment since graduation from Police College, and everything in front of him screamed felony. It was manslaughter at least, perhaps murder, and maybe — no, for sure — robbery as well. He reached for the radio in his belt but then stopped. He'd been here just a couple of minutes. One or two more wouldn't really matter all that much. Not to the dead man on the floor, anyway. Besides, one more check wouldn't hurt. There was no way he was going to make a mistake on this one. His first big one!

"Young man!" Cam was startled out of his inner dialogue by a whiny, high-pitched voice. Bentley Threndyle didn't pull punches. "Are you going to call your whatever person as the other officer told you, or are you just going to stand there? Perhaps you like watching poor Morton bleed?"

Cam looked at the body of Morton Threndyle, then turned uneasily back to the owner of the whiny voice. Bentley's appearance was a counterpoint to the haughtiness of his manner, for he was covered with spilled paint. There was paint in his sandy-gray hair and on his gold-rimmed glasses, paint all over the carefully pressed tweed jacket and down the right side of his wheelchair. Blobs still clinging to his knees were trickling slowly down his pantlegs into the cuffs and filling the creases in his shoes. Even the end of his tie, which stuck out beneath the jacket, had paint on it. Bentley Threndyle was a study in Cardona Ivory 2884. Cam had already written the paint color into his notebook. He didn't know why, but he thought it could be important later.

The interior of Threndyle Brothers Inc., "Specialists in Art and Furnishings of the Georgian Period," was in the midst of a renovation. The painters had gone on a lunch break before the shooting occurred and had left open cans of paint on the scaffold that now stood perilously askew above the body on the floor. It was during the struggle between Morton and the intruder, according to Bentley, that the paint had been knocked over.

Morton, too, or rather his body, was covered in spilled paint. In fact he was lying face down in a pool of Cardona Ivory, his blood making little patterns and puddles in it like a child's first attempt at drawing a map. A twisting red trail had almost encircled the body from the sandy-gray hair to the almost-white sneakers. It was like an incomprehensible modern painting, Cam had thought when he first saw the scene. Very much out of place in this store!

Threndyle Brothers Inc. was one of a kind. It was a key business in a street of very trendy, extremely expensive boutiques, although off-the-street business represented only a tiny fraction of the Threndyle income. Most of it came from extensive and complex international dealings on behalf of a stable of wealthy clients. Twins Morton and Bentley, like their father and grandfather, were counted among the principal antique dealers on the continent.

Only minutes before, Cam and his partner had heard shots — two of them — as they were walking down the street. They'd only just passed the Threndyle store. Neither had looked in. There was nothing to see,

ken
WEBER

what with all the antiques covered by canvas sheets. The store was closed for renovations, and besides, like everyone else in an official or responsible capacity, police officers avoided the Threndyle twins. They were grouchy and rich and influential. Both were well known, though, favorites of the local media, partly because they were absolutely identical except for one thing: Bentley couldn't walk.

"Nothing! Not a trace! The guy had to know beforehand where to go!" Cam's partner came blustering through the back door. "I checked the alley both ways. No sign." He stepped carefully around the body. The blood and paint were starting to work their way toward a corner now. "Too bad some of the paint didn't hit him, too. Might have left some tracks. Did you call in? The boss'll want to be here himself for this one, I'd bet."

"I…uh…was just about to." Cam swallowed, quietly, he hoped. He was very nervous. "Just wanted to make sure first that we didn't miss anything."

"What's there to miss?" The other policeman asked. He was puffing a bit and his voice was loud enough to make Cam just a bit defensive.

Bentley Threndyle didn't help either. "Yes, call! I already told you what happened!" He rolled the wheelchair backward so abruptly it almost hit the scaffold. "I told you!" he repeated. "The painters weren't gone five minutes when this, this…person came right through the back door. I know it's supposed to be locked all the time, but it wasn't. Morton was going to set out the garbage."

Cam almost spoke then checked himself. When they heard the shots and came running, the front door had been unlocked, too. As they burst in to find Morton on the floor, and Bentley leaning from the wheelchair holding his brother's wrist, Cam had seen the back door was wide open. He hadn't known about the garbage.

"He came right through the door," Bentley continued. "Right behind poor Morton. I told you all this already! He had this gun and he and Morton began to fight. That's why there's paint all over. Then he shot. Two times! Poor Morton! By the time you got here, the man was out and gone! Look. How much longer do I have to sit here and look at Morton. I can't do anything now. You can tell your whatever person to talk to me at home!"

As he began to turn the wheelchair toward the front door, Cam finally took the radio off his belt.

"You stay here!" he said with a firmness that made the two other men look at him with surprise. "You stay here," he said again. "Right in my sight until a doctor examines you."

Why does Cam Lindsey want the Threndyle twin to "stay right here" until he is examined by a doctor?

Solution below

solutions/answers

Solution to "Two Shots in the Antique Store"

Cam Lindsay feels that the twin in the wheelchair, who supposedly is Bentley Threndyle, may really be Morton. Bentley cannot walk. Morton can. Although the two are identical twins and can't be told apart, the one who walks would naturally have creases in his shoes. Cam noticed that the Cardona Ivory 2884 that ran down the twin's legs as he sat in the wheelchair, also ran into the creases in his shoes.

Answers to "Pen-Free Puzzle Posers (Easy)"

Addition: The answer is 3,100. When you leave the john, read this aloud rapidly to others about you and have them add mentally. Over half will answer 4,000.

The crewpersons crawled through the culvert under Mono Cliff Road at different times.

At Rockwood cranberry bog, by working cooperatively, the workers double the amount in a basket every second. Thus, if they fill a basket every minute, it is half full at 59 seconds.

Answers to "Pen-Free Puzzle Posers (Challenge)"

Saneya first fills the eight-quart container to the top, then pours into the seven-quart container until it is full. This leaves one quart of water in the eight. She empties out the seven-quart container and then pours the one quart into it. She fills the eight-quart container again, pours as much as she can into the seven, leaving two quarts in the eight this time. Once more she empties out the seven, and then puts the two quarts into it. This time, when she fills the eight-quart container and pours as much as she can from it into the seven, there will be three quarts left.

The number 6 occurs twenty times.

ken
WEBER

Vera smoked twenty-one cigarettes. The sixteen she had at the time of her promise yielded sixteen butts, which were rolled into four cigarettes. These four yielded four more butts for a single, final smoke.

Answers to "Trick or Treat"

1. Casper the Friendly Ghost (Nightmare is a horseghost.) 2. Dracula. (Vlad's method of execution — impaling victims alive on sharpened stakes — did not originate with him. It was established practice in the area, especially for groups of captured soldiers.) 3. Lady Godiva, during her famous ride through Coventry. In the legend, the villagers agreed not to look, but Tom did and was blinded for his trouble. 4. United Nations International Children's Emergency Fund (more often the U.N. Children's Fund) 5. None (four nominations) 6. The guitar. This was a promo gimmick for Elvis Presley before he hit the big time. 7. Frankenstein. (By the year 2000, movies about Frankenstein outnumbered movies about Dracula 160-112!) 8. Oz. It's the Wizard of Oz's full name. 9. Work. If you have it, you probably have eosophobia (fear of dawn), too.

Answers to "Let There Be Peace"

1. Pearson, Prime Minister of Canada; Brandt, Chancellor of West Germany; Begin, Prime Minister of Israel; Walesa, President of Poland. The others: Bunche (U.S. diplomat), Schweitzer (humanitarian), Hammarskjold (Sec.-Gen. of the UN), Sakharov (Russian peace activist), Tutu (South African bishop), Lama (Tibetan king/spiritual leader) 2. In a railroad car, near the palace of Versailles in France. 3. Calumet. (a *calpac* is a hat, and a *caltrop* is a weapon) 4. Canada 5. Pax 6. "Hark! The Herald Angels Sing" 7. United Nations main building 8. Sons 9. Henri Dunant is the founder of the Red Cross. (Passy founded the International League of Peace in 1868.)

Answers to "Old Time Rock-and-Roll"

1. Their name. The Stones took it from one of Muddy Waters' songs, "Rolling Stone Blues." 2. Eric Clapton 3. It was slang for sex, used especially by black people. 4. It was the title Julian Lennon gave to a piece of his own art. His father, John, said the work was his inspiration for the song. 5. Presley, 29, over the Beatles' 22 6. Bruce Springsteen 7. Don Maclean 8. Jerry Lee Lewis 9. Elton John

Answers to "Hands-Free Word Adventure: I always forget how to spell that"

desiccate	consensus
anisette	license
privilege	accommodate
ukulele	supersede
separate	rhythm
pursuant	removable
attachment	antiseptic
commiserate	committee
heterogeneous	prodigious
combustible	optimism

Answers to "Hands-Free Word Adventure: You know more Latin than you realize"

1. f, 2. d, 3. i, 4. h, 5. g, 6. a, 7. c, 8. b, 9. j 10. e. (Pushtu and Dzongkha are official languages of Afghanistan and Bhutan respectively.)

section THREE

emerge informed

And now for a division in scholarly etymological opinion. The expression "the real McCoy" comes from Prohibition Era rumrunner Bill McCoy, who supposedly shipped genuine (as opposed to homebrewed) rum from Canada down the Atlantic coast to the U.S. *Or*, it comes from lightweight boxer Kid McCoy (Norman Selby, 1873-1940). McCoy bonked a drunk who refused to believe he was indeed the boxer. When the drunk came to, his first words were, "You're the real McCoy, all right."

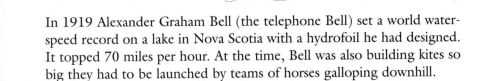

In 1919 Alexander Graham Bell (the telephone Bell) set a world water-speed record on a lake in Nova Scotia with a hydrofoil he had designed. It topped 70 miles per hour. At the time, Bell was also building kites so big they had to be launched by teams of horses galloping downhill.

One of Shakespeare's most successful competitors for audience ratings in Elizabethan England was an exceptionally talented horse named Marocco. This unusual equine could wow the crowds with acts like returning a glove to its owner after the proper name was whispered in his ear. Marocco could also tap out the correct number of pence in a silver coin. (Roy Rogers' Trigger did a similar schtick in his act.) Unfortunately, Marocco's owner took him on tour. He was a hit in Austria and in France, but the Inquisition in Italy was not impressed. Both Marocco and his owner were found to be diabolically inspired and were burned at the stake in Rome.

Gertrude and Leo Stein paid $30 for their first Picasso, and from 1906 to 1909 had the entire Picasso market cornered. Not by design. It was because no one else wanted any! At the time, Picasso was burning some of his work to keep warm. He couldn't afford to pay for fuel.

shifts of wit

During a recital in Munich in 1936, pianist Artur Schnabel was barely into the vigorous first movement of Beethoven's "Emperor" concerto when he noticed an elderly lady in the front row had fallen asleep. She slept soundly through all three movements but snapped awake with a start in the ovation that followed. As the lengthy applause continued to fill the concert hall, Schnabel leaned over to her and whispered, "Sorry about the applause, madame. I played as softly as I could."

Television personality Garry Moore was presented an award for spontaneity in 1961 and brought the house down by facetiously paying tribute to "the four guys responsible for my spontaneity — my writers." Moore was followed to the stage by the next award winner, Bishop Fulton J. Sheen. "I also want to pay tribute to my four writers," the bishop said. "Matthew, Mark, Luke and John."

Groucho Marx was asked by the National Teachers Association to put in a plug for reading on his television show if he could, especially for reading books. Shortly after, Marx signed off with, "Remember. Outside of a dog, a man's best friend is a book. Inside of a dog, it's too dark to read."

Although the collection of things that Yogi Berra never said continues to grow, there is, nevertheless, at least one comment by the former Yankees catcher for which provenance is certain, because a stadium full of people heard it, all at the same time. On "Yogi Berra" day in his hometown of St. Louis, Berra began his acceptance speech with, "I want to thank all the people who made this night necessary."

A student conductor was privileged to meet with composer Richard Strauss before leading the Bavarian Symphony through his *Also Sprach Zarathustra*. To the young man's request for advice, Strauss's response was, "Don't look at the brass. It only encourages them."

British actor Robert Morley paid a visit to an old friend and fellow actor, Llewellyn Rees, who had been retired and out of the public eye for quite some time.

"Kind of you to visit," said Rees. "Nice to see old friends. A lot of people think I'm dead."

"Not if they look closely," said Morley.

 # not their finest hour

"X-rays will prove to be a hoax," stated William Thomas, Lord Kelvin, during his term as president of the Royal Society (1890–95). While in office, he is also credited with this prediction: "Radio has no future."

Lord Kelvin is not alone. Thomas Edison had hired a bright young Canadian physicist, Reginald Fessenden, who in 1897 wanted to experiment with wireless broadcasting of the human voice. "Fessie," Edison said to him, "what do you say are man's chances of jumping over the moon? I think that one is as likely as the other." Fessenden made the first radio broadcast on December 23, 1900.

"Man will not fly for 50 years," estimated Wilbur Wright, brother of Orville, in 1901. (At the time of this statement, Gustave Whitehead had made a well-documented and witnessed powered flight of half a mile, on August 14, in Fairfield, Connecticut. A Frenchman, Clement Ader, had made a powered flight even earlier, in 1890. Contrary to popular belief, the Wrights were not the first to achieve powered flight.)

ken
WEBER

"[Television] won't be able to hold on to any market it captures after the first six months. People will soon get tired of staring at a plywood box," said Darryl F. Zanuck in 1946.

"The Americans have need of the telephone, but we do not. We have plenty of office boys," announced William Preece, Chief Engineer, British Post Office, in 1876. (At the time of the invention of the telephone, construction technology was capable of putting up multi-story buildings, but rarely did office buildings exceed four stories, as that was the efficiency limit for both office-boy runners and vacuum-tube systems, the two means by which inter-office memos got around.)

U.S. Patent Office Director Charles Duell declared in 1899, "Everything that can be invented has been invented."

trivia test

Gimme a T!

T-names for your child: Tabitha (from Greek, meaning "gazelle"); Tammy (from Hebrew, meaning "perfection"); Tania (from Russian, meaning "fairy princess"); Theresa (from Greek, meaning "reaper"); Trixie (from Latin, a variation of Beatrix, meaning "she who makes others happy"); Talbot (from Old French, meaning "pillager"); Telford (from Old French, meaning "iron-cutter"); Ted (for Theodore, from Greek, meaning "gift of God"); Thomas and Timothy (from Greek, meaning "twin" and "honoring God," respectively); Todd (from Old English/Gaelic, meaning "fox"); Trevor (from Gaelic, meaning "wise"); Tyler (from Middle English, meaning "roofer").

1. Captain James T. Kirk of the starship *Enterprise*. What does the T stand for?

2. What substance is made by the nitration of toluene with sulfuric and nitric acids?

3. The *Tonight Show:* Johnny Carson's long tenure as host began in 1962 (for trivia buffs: he was introduced on his first night by Groucho Marx). Jay Leno followed Johnny. Who were the two regular hosts prior to Johnny?

4. What's a "teetotaler"? What's a "teetotum"?

5. The following sports have been medal events in the Summer Olympics: trap shooting, tug of war, triple jump, tornado (yacht) race. Which, if any, have been discontinued?

6. "Tutti-frutti" was sung by Little Richard. It's also sold by Baskin-Robbins. "Tutti-frutti" is an Italian phrase. What does it mean?

7. Sesame Street star Kermit is officially Kermit T. Frog. What does the T stand for in his name?

8. How many sovereign countries can you name that begin with the letter T? At the time this book was published, eleven of these were in the UN.

9. Ingrid Bergman, Helen Hayes, Liza Minelli and others are called TOE winners in media jargon, because of three different awards they have won. What are the awards?

10. Strictly for total trivia buffs: In the phrase "to a T," what does the T stand for?

Answers on page 85

this could take a minute, so be sure there's no one waiting

"It Looketh Like a Silly Game"

The first Olympic medals for golf were awarded in 1900. (In men's competition, the U.S.A. won gold; Great Britain took silver and bronze; for women it was U.S.A. gold, Switzerland silver, and Great Britain bronze.) That golf was chosen as a medal event as the modern Olympics got under way was not surprising, for by the beginning of the twentieth century, it was a well-established sport, having been around for some 150 years. Or 300 years. Or possibly 450. Or maybe even 500. And if there are any takers, 1,800 and 2,100 years are on offer too.

The Chinese make what seems to be the earliest claim for the game. Illustrations dating back several centuries before Christ show what can be interpreted as some form of stick-hitting-a-ball type of sport. In the early days of the Roman Empire (this is the 1,800-year claim) legionnaires enjoyed a game called *paganica*. It was played with a bent wooden stick and a leather ball filled with feathers, and the troops may well have brought the pastime with them to "Britannica" in 55 A.D. Still another claim, a reasonable one, goes to the Low Countries, where a game called *kolven* also used a ball and bent stick. The Dutch played it on ice, trying to putt the ball at a stake, croquet-style, though in woodcut illustrations from Belgium dating around the same time (1500s) players are quite clearly trying to putt the ball into a hole.

Although other claims abound (at the height of the Cold War, the Soviet Union, for reasons it never explained, insisted that golf originated in Denmark in the fifteenth century), the most clearly traceable origins of what we understand as the modern game of golf began in Scotland. Not complimentary traces either. The first reference is a 1457 decree ordering that the game be "utterly *cryit doun* and *nocht usit!*" because it interfered with mandatory archery practice. It was forbidden again in 1471, in an ordinance that also outlawed the playing of *"futebal,"* and one more time, in 1491. On this latter occasion, fines and other punishments were stipulated.

Unquestionably, golf was more appealing to the good citizens of Scotland than the work they were supposed to be doing.

The 1491 edict was the work of Scottish King James IV, who based his decision partly on the impression that it "looketh like a silly game." His attitude must have been a pretty soft one, though, for at the end of James's reign, accounting records of the Lord High Treasurer show the purchase of golf balls and other equipment for the "pleysure of His Majestye." The king's son, James V, became an avid golfer, and his granddaughter, the legendary Mary, Queen of Scots, was so keen she was out on the links only a few days after her husband was strangled outside Edinburgh in 1567. Thus, by 1592, restrictions on playing golf were imposed only on Sundays. And just a few years after that, authorities eased the prohibition even further. In what seems to be a remarkably modern-day position, the law was softened so golfers could flail away at any time, even on Sundays — except during sermons.

The Scottish royal family took golf south when it united with the English throne in 1603. James VI, who went to London to be James I, appointed the first royal clubmaker. In 1685, his grandson, James II, established royal precedent for what would become another golfing tradition. He challenged a pair of Scottish noblemen to a match, and for his partner, chose a commoner by the name of Johne Patersone. Although there is no proof, Patersone had to be a ringer, for he and the king won handily, though James was widely known to be a duffer. (Patersone, a shoemaker, bought a big house in London a week after the match.)

Over the next century, the popularity of the sport grew rapidly. The Royal and Ancient Golf Club of St. Andrews was founded in 1754 (it is still a public course, with remarkably low green fees!). England's first club, the Royal Blackheath, opened in 1787. Although there were no courses yet in North America, an ad for equipment in a New York paper in 1779 suggests that more than one cow pasture was finding alternate uses. The first course in North America was laid out in Montreal, predating the first one in the U.S. by some 15 years. In 1888 the first American course opened, a six-hole affair in Yonkers, New York.

By this time, the game was gradually becoming standardized into its present form. The 18-hole system was established by St. Andrews as early as 1764. Originally, the St. Andrews course had been laid out with a phenomenal lack of forward planning, for it had 11 holes in a straight line along the seacoast. Since golfers wanted to play their way back, as well as out (thus playing a "round") it's not hard to figure out why problems might develop on a busy day. Gutta percha balls, called "gutties," replaced leather balls in the 1850s, despite the fact the new type tended to slice and hook. They were considered much better than the leather ones, which were virtually unplayable when wet. Before long, someone noticed that an older "guttie," one with pocks and chips from previous use, flew straighter than a new one, so that by the end of the decade all golf balls acquired "dimples" (332 per ball). The rubber-cored ball made its appearance in 1898, and the tapered wooden tee the following year.

Thus, by the time the first Olympic medals were awarded for golf, the sport was very much the type of game we know today — without the green jackets. Unfortunately, it lasted for only two sets at the Olympics, 1900 and 1904, because in London, in 1908, the British entrants threw such a hissy fit that the event was dropped. Still, golf showed that in the beginning, anyway, the Olympics really were an amateur contest. In 1900, in Paris, the U.S. took gold for the ladies' event, but winner Margaret Abbott later acknowledged she won because most of the other entrants showed up in high heels, whalebone corsets and tight skirts, with only the barest notion of how to play the game.

In 1904, in St. Louis, the women didn't show up at all, but the men's play was a dramatic center of attention. The gold medal was considered a shoo-in for U.S. champion Chandler Egan, but he was trounced by the Canadian entrant, George Seymour Lyon. Entirely unorthodox in both personal manner and style of play, Lyon was criticized by American papers for his "coal heaver's swing," and for his behavior on the course, where he would do handstands while awaiting his turn on the tee. As though to prove a point, at the medal ceremonies Lyon walked to the presentation stand on his hands to receive the gold. Four years later, at the 1908 Olympics in London, when the Americans did not show and the British golfers withdrew, Lyon was offered the gold by default, but he turned it down, showing more than a little class in a game that considers such things important.

hands-free word adventure

Oh, no! Not more puns!

The trouble with paranomasiphiles is that they never stop. It takes only a few successful puns to turn them into paranomasiacs. Still, there should be just enough samples below to satisfy the habit without making anyone go on a bender.

Match each word below with its appropriate paranomasic explanation.

appear	the absolute truth
brotherhood	the first thing you see on a '59 DeSoto
cadence	member of the House of Lords
cantaloupe	boycott of Dubble Bubble
denounce	parts of speech (like deverbs, etc.)
drivel	the crook in your family
eureka	you don't look too good either
gumption	hot tip at the track
intense	light rain and mift
misconduct	can't get engaged either
noble	worn in Minnesota on wet days
paraffins	where campers sleep
robbers	thtrings around garbage bagth
sherbet	why Kay always flunks
tithe	what you do if you're on page 7 and the orchestra's on page 8

Answers on page 86

ken
WEBER

emerge informed

Although you won't find this in the *Guinness Book of World Records,* the record for the largest naval fleet ever captured by a troop of cavalry goes to French general Charles Pichegru. On January 20, 1794, during a foray deep into the Netherlands, Pichegru and his men came to the outskirts of Amsterdam and found the Dutch fleet frozen solidly into the harbor ice. He was able to capture the entire fleet with a troop of hussars.

For those who are titillated by polysyllabic sesquipedalianism: the longest word recorded in standard dictionaries is pneumonoultramicroscopicsilicovolcanoconiosis. It appears in Webster's Third, among others, and is the name of a lung disease. A contender is floccinaucinihilipilification (the act of rendering worthless).

Try not to think of this the next time you listen to J. S. Bach. Near the end of his life he was strapped down on two separate occasions to have his eyes operated on by English surgeon John Taylor. No anesthetic. It was unknown at the time. The procedure was to force several quarts of some inebriate down the throat of the patient and then leave him — and his eyes — to the mercy of the surgeon's lancet. Both operations (no surprise here) were failures. Taylor also failed when he strapped down and tried his skills on Handel a few years later.

Santayana's Apothegm: "A fanatic is one who redoubles his effort when he's forgotten his aim."

Every year since 1893 has seen a Stanley Cup final. Except 1919. That year, despite the fact the Spanish Flu pandemic had closed many public arenas in North America, the Montreal Canadiens journeyed west to take on the Seattle Metropolitans. After two wins apiece and a tie, the series was shut down because several Canadiens were hospitalized with the flu. One of their stars, "Bad" Joe Hall, died of it.

shifts of wit

"To have the proper effect with the needle rather than the sword is an art form all its own."

Marsha Penner (The *Toronto Sun* is a tabloid-style daily newspaper.)

"I wouldn't exactly say that readers of the *Sun* have intellectual limitations, but I do know that most of the letters to the editor are written with crayons."

George Burns, upon being asked how it felt to have bypass surgery.

"Not as bad as playing Akron."

At Vancouver International Airport, as HRH Prince Philip stepped to the tarmac…

Premier Bennett: "And how was your flight, sir?"
HRH: "Have you ever flown?"
Premier Bennett: "Oh, yes, often."
HRH: "Well, it was like that."

Raffaello Sanzio (Raphael, 1483-1520) was brought to Rome from Florence in 1508 by Pope Julius II. His first commission, to paint a number of frescoes, was regularly hindered by criticism from a pair of cardinals. According to diaries of the account, the interference disappeared after the following exchange.

Their Eminences: "The face of the apostle Paul is far too red."
Raphael: "He blushes to see into whose hands the church has fallen."

"All Ireland is washed by the Gulf Stream. Except my wife's family."

Editor Paul Fisher, Methuen Publications, rejecting an unsolicited manuscript

"I am returning this paper. Someone has written on it."

At the same publishing house, a memo to Fisher from F.D. Wardle asked of yet another unsolicited manuscript, "Think this would work if it had more fire in it?" To which Fisher replied,

"I rather think the opposite."

pen-free puzzle posers
(MODERATE)

1. Before you lies a pile of solid, red cubes made of plastic, each measuring exactly one inch on all sides.

   a) How many of these cubes will you need to build a solid cube measuring three inches on all sides?

   b) How many 3" x 3" flat surfaces does the large cube have?

   c) If all the outside edges of the large cube were laid out in a straight, unbroken line, how many inches long would it be?

2. Imagine now that the large cube has been painted white on all sides.

   a) How many of the small cubes used to construct the large cube will be white on two sides only?

   b) How many of the small cubes will be white on one side only?

   c) How many of the small cubes will not have any white at all?

   d) How many will be white on three sides?

3. Now imagine that each corner (the intersection of three outside edges) has been filed down to make new flat surfaces. These flat surfaces have sides of exactly equal length.

a) How many edges are there on each filed surface?

b) After the filing, how many flat surfaces are there on the outside of the large cube?

c) After the filing, how many separate edges are there on the outside of the large cube?

d) What is the total number of corners now on the large cube?

Answers on page 86

going out in style...philosophically

"Only one man understood me, and he didn't understand me." The final words of philosopher Georg Wilhelm Friedrich Hegel in 1831. (It helps to appreciate Hegel's comment if you understand that his principal hypothesis was that truth is achieved only when you posit something and then deny it, thus combining two half-truths in a synthesis which contains a greater portion of truth in its complexity.) There weren't many people at the bedside when Hegel passed on.

You would expect something erudite from scholarly Morris Berg, who studied a dozen languages and maintained a wide range of academic interests. His final line in 1972: "How did the Mets do today?"

Berg certainly must have appreciated the exit line of Baseball Hall of Famer Michael Kelly (Reds, Cubs, Braves, Giants). In 1894 Kelly was taken to hospital suffering from pneumonia. As he was transferred from a stretcher to a bed he commented, "This is my last slide."

Apparently, Kelly was expecting to go, unlike the famous Greek mathematician Archimedes (of "Archimedes Principle" fame). Archimedes was concentrating on a problem in 212 B.C., oblivious to the fact that an invading army was burning the city around him. "Don't disturb the circles!" he said to the soldier who broke into his house. Unfortunately, the soldier had no appreciation whatever of mathematics and killed Archimedes on the spot.

French encyclopedist Denis Diderot was not expecting to go either, in 1784. When he reached for an apricot at dinner, his wife told him not to eat it. His last words: "How in the devil can it hurt me?"

If nothing else, Diderot's departure line lacks the clear precision in that of former New York mayor Abram S. Hewitt in 1903. On his hospital bed, Hewitt took the oxygen tube out of his mouth and made the following announcement: "And now I am officially dead." And a few minutes later he was.

Hewitt's resolve was somewhat firmer, perhaps, than that of Bertrand Russell (1872-1970), who, when asked if he would be prepared to die for his beliefs, replied, "Of course not. After all, I may be wrong."

Russell lived for several years after that, but as a near-the-end comment, it's a gem. For that category, however, first prize goes to French composer Daniel Auber, who, at age 89 attended a funeral of a friend and told his fellow mourners, "I believe this is the last time I'll take part as an amateur."

trivia test

You Can't Have One Without the Other (Famous Pairs)

In 1903 there was Orville and Wilbur. Orville flew the plane first while Wilbur watched. Of comedians Rowan and Martin, Dan Rowan smoked a pipe and looked cynical while Dick clowned around. Comic books had Mutt and Jeff. Mutt was the tall one. In the Currier and Ives partnership, it was Nathaniel Currier who first got the business going and brought Frederick Ives in. The Roadrunner and the Coyote are a well-known pair, even though Wile E. was paired with Ralph the sheepdog at first. Perhaps the tastiest pair — and the most colorful, because they don't melt in your hand — is M & Ms. (That's M for Mars, the chocolate bar company, and M for Merrie, the chemist who came up with the idea in 1941.)

1. Gilbert & Sullivan: which one wrote the music?

2. Jekyll & Hyde: which one was the bad guy?

3. Harry Longbaugh & George Parker: which one was the Sundance Kid?

4. Right eye/left eye: on which did Mr. Peanut wear the monocle?

5. Livingstone & Stanley: which one explored the Congo River?

6. Seigfreid & Roy: which one is the blonde?

7. Laurel & Hardy: which one was born in the U.S.?

8. Phil & Tony Esposito: which one was the goalie?

9. Mason & Dixon: which one was the other's assistant?

10. Chip 'n' Dale: which one has a pink nose and is not too bright?

11. Dick and Tom Smothers: which one played the bass viol?

12. Dear Ann & Dear Abby: which twin is Pauline Esther, and which one is Esther Pauline?

Answers on page 85

emerge informed

Canada's province of Manitoba was the first jurisdiction in North America to use numbers to identify highways. That was in 1920. Before that time it was customary to paint colored bands on fenceposts to assure drivers they were still on the right road. Also in Manitoba, until 1959, it was illegal to drink beer in a privy.

Switzerland is the world leader in per capita consumption of chocolate. That's where chocolate fit for eating was first perfected in 1876, though Europeans were drinking the stuff long before this. A drink of chocolate was long thought to be an aphrodisiac, in part because the great Aztec king Montezuma was known to down a cup each time he visited his harem. In fact, chocolate does contain a mild stimulant known as theobromine (as well as caffeine). Theoretically, then, population growth in Switzerland should be outpacing the rest of the world, but that's not what's happening.

Educational supply catalogues in Britain no longer offer canes (for caning, of course) but still did so in the 1970s. Legitimate availability seems to have had little impact on the purchasing agent for City of London schools, however. In 1977 a London councilman revealed that the school authority was buying its canes from a sex shop that had already been raided twice that year by police.

To shoot a hole-in-one in golf is ten times easier than rolling a perfect 300 game in ten-pin bowling says *Compendium of Odds*. The bowler's odds are 300,000 to 1, while the golfer enjoys 30,000 to 1. James Cash, from Nebraska, didn't know this when he put his tee shot right to the edge of the cup on a course in Belmont, Massachusetts, one sunny day in 1929. As he walked down the fairway, an earth tremor, one of three recorded that day, shook the green and the ball dropped in. (Which for golf brings the odds down to 29,999 to 1 during earthquakes.)

for deposit in your "one-up" account

Drop these in when appropriate (or even when not appropriate)!

Venetian blinds were invented in Japan

Shakespeare's *A Midsummer Night's Dream* is set in the early spring.

Catgut on tennis rackets (mostly synthetic now) was actually sheep gut.

The game we call Chinese Checkers was invented in Sweden.

Banana oil is actually a chemical compound, amyl acetate.

A ten gallon hat holds just under three-quarters of a gallon.

Oktoberfest in Munich begins in September.

Aaron Copeland's "Appalachian Spring" premiered in the fall of 1944.

Thomas Lanier "Tennessee" Williams was born in Mississippi.

Johann Strauss Jr., known as "the waltz king," never learned how to waltz.

John Quincy Adams, not James Monroe, wrote the Monroe Doctrine.

The sides of the warship *Old Ironsides* (1797) were wooden.

Camel-hair brushes (the "genuine" kind) are made of fur from squirrels.

Ulysses S. Grant is not buried in Grant's Tomb. (To be technical, he's entombed there. No one dug a grave and buried him.)

hands-free
word adventures

If you can read this, then you can spell...

Miss King always tried valiantly to interest her students in current affairs, but somehow her efforts were always sidetracked by unexpected questions. For example, one day early in her teaching career, she seized upon a media frenzy created by the visit of Russian premier Nikita Krushchev and his wife to North America. But her lesson was immediately diverted when Lucy, perched as usual at the edge of the group, asked, "What color is fuschia? The TV said Mrs. Khrushev's dress was fuschia."

Miss King wrote "f u s c h i a" on the chalkboard and then passed Lucy a dictionary.

"Perhaps you could look it up for us," she said, and returned to the subject of Premier and Mrs. Khrushchev and their state visit.

After a few moments, Lucy piped up, "It's not in this dictionary."

"It must be!" Miss King was insistent. "Did you look up...wait a minute. Try it this way!" This time she wrote "f u c h s i a" on the chalkboard, and Lucy soon found it.

That was the day Miss King learned to spell fuchsia. She had been recognizing the word in print for years but had never really paid attention to it. Being the good teacher she was, she looked up the derivation of the word and found that the fuchsia is a flower named after German botanist Leonard Fuchs, and that the reddish-purple color is named after the flower. On the very next day Miss King built a spelling lesson around the experience.

"Two things we must always do with an unusual word, class," she said. "First, look at the word. Really see it! Then come up with an association or idea to remember it better. Now that I've really looked and have an association, I'll never get fuchsia wrong again!"

Without looking at the text above, spell the surname of the Russian premier.

Answer on page 86

pen-free puzzle posers
(CHALLENGE)

1. Long before the arrival of the first Europeans, some of the Inuit people living in the Arctic had developed an effective technique for hunting seals, one of their principal sources of food, clothing and tools.

Seals were caught by harpooning them at their breathing holes in the ice. To be able to do this an Innuit hunter would stand right at one of these holes, knowing that seals return to a hole regularly, both to breathe and to keep ice from forming and closing it. The Inuit hunters had learned over generations that seals will instinctively avoid a breathing hole if they hear noises around it. From experience, the hunters also knew that seals must have incredibly sharp hearing underwater, for the sound of a pair of a footsteps going to and stopping at a breathing hole is enough to cause them to abandon the spot and allow it to freeze over.

What technique did the Innuit hunters develop to circumvent the problem?

2. Some interesting problems in basic arithmetic. These can all be solved using the addition, subtraction, multiplication and division skills you learned before the fourth grade (or, if you weren't paying attention, by the seventh grade).

Arrange three 6s so that they equal 7.

Arrange three 4s so that they equal 11.

Arrange four 9s so that they equal 100.

Arrange four 3s so that they equal 24.

3. After stealing a sealed bag of one-carat industrial diamonds, three thieves hid out in a cheap motel room. Waiting, however, was more difficult for them than stealing, and before long the three were squabbling. On the second night, one of the thieves waited until the other two were asleep, silently broke the seal, and taking her third out of the bag, slipped out the door. Unbeknownst to her, one of partners was awake and watching, and as soon as she was gone, that partner got up, counted out what he thought was his third and, like the first thief, disappeared. The third thief had actually been asleep. After an hour he awoke and, completely unaware of what had happened, or even that his partners were gone, silently counted out what he thought was his one third of the loot and stole outside. Early the next morning, the motel owner found a bag in the room, with eight one-carat industrial diamonds in it.

How many diamonds were in the bag when the thieves first got to the motel?

Answers on page 86

 trivia test

Along the World's Longest Unguarded Border

It could be that the world's longest unguarded border — not to mention the world's longest border, period — remains unguarded for reasons like this: On a warm June afternoon in 1812, American officers on a visit to the Canadian side were profoundly embarrassed to learn they were at war with their hosts. Seems they had rowed across the border (the Niagara River) for tea with officers at Fort George, and a courier from York (now Toronto) burst in with the news that the U.S. had declared war on Canada. These American officers did not get confirmation from their own side for another week because the U.S. War Department chose to inform their post, Fort Niagara, by mail.

1. What Canadian provinces do not make physical land contact with the U.S.?

2. How many U.S. states and Canadian provinces have all straight line borders? four? five? six? seven?

3. Using strict cartography principles, what Canadian provinces and U.S. states can be said to have Atlantic coastlines? (Only the main Atlantic itself is used in this procedure; gulfs, bays and straits are excluded.)

4. Which of the following is mispelled: Saskatchewan? Missouri? North West Territories?

5. How many U.S. states have four-letter names?

6. Which Canadian province was named after a British princess? Which U.S. state was named after a British king?

7. What Canadian province borders on the largest number of other provinces? What two U.S states border on the largest number of other states?

8. What Canadian provinces and U.S. states have coastlines on the Great Lakes?

9. Of the five vowels, A, E, I, O, U, which is the only one that does not begin a Canadian provincial or U.S. state name?

10. How many U.S. states and Canadian provinces have names that end in the letter A?

Answers on page 85

 shifts of wit

At a civic reception in Ottawa in 1952, the city's mayor, Charlotte Whitton, was hosting the Lord Mayor of London. Whitton, at the time one of the world's very few woman mayors of a major city, modestly wore a rose on the front of her dress. On the Lord Mayor's chest dangled his huge chain of office. After several martinis, his worship bent over the tiny Whitton and asked, "If I smell your rose, will you blush?" To which she replied, "If I pull your chain, will you flush?"

More questions that have led elsewhere...

To Zsa Zsa Gabor:
> "How many husbands have you had?"
> "You mean apart from my own?"

To boxer Jack Sharkey (after an early round KO):
> "How come you hit him when he wasn't looking?"
> "What was I supposed to do, mail him a letter?"

To Charlie Chaplin (when he came in third in a Charlie Chaplin look-alike contest in Monte Carlo):
> "How do you account for this?"
> "Maybe it was my mustache?"

To critic Oskar Blumenthal after a failed premiere:
> "If it was so bad, why didn't the audience hiss?"
> "You can't hiss and yawn at the same time."

To Mohandas Gandhi:
> "What do you think of western civilization?"
> "I think that it would be a very good idea."

To John Barrymore:
> "What do you think of Prohibition?"
> "Fortunately, I don't think of it."

To President Jimmy Carter, from a reporter (while on a trip to India, he was taken to an experimental site where methane gas was being collected from a pit of cow manure):
> "If I fell in, Mr. President, you'd pull me out, wouldn't you?"
> "Certainly. After a suitable interval."

emerge informed

For several centuries in North America, "jay" was a slang term for clod or hick. A "jay walker" — before police started issuing tickets for the practice — was simply an unsophisticated person walking about the streets in mild amazement.

George III of England had a very loving relationship with his wife, Queen Charlotte, notwithstanding his habit of carrying on extended conversations with individual trees in the park at Windsor. It's now believed his "madness" came either from porphyria or from lead poisoning gradually accumulated from the cooking vessels used to prepare his two favorite foods, sauerkraut and lemonade.

NASA's first way-out-in-space launch was the Voyager Project, a multiple-planet flyby of two Mariner spacecraft in 1977. The idea was to take advantage of a celestial alignment of Jupiter, Saturn, Uranus and Neptune that occurs once every 175 years. Aboard the craft, just in case, were many different samples of Earth's ingenuity, including recorded music. Chosen to represent rock-and-roll for any extraterrestrials that happened to tune in was Chuck Berry singing "Johnny B. Goode."

September 1951: Hamilton, Bermuda. Residents — those who weren't evacuated — were bracing for the worst hurricane since records were kept. When the storm was about 10 miles offshore, it was overtaken by another hurricane that came up right behind it. Meteorologists were even more surprised than the first hurricane was, but no one in Bermuda complained of the outcome. The clash of the two forces caused both to weaken and turn out to sea.

In 1620 the *Mayflower* deposited her cargo of pilgrims on the shores of Cape Cod Bay, not at Plymouth Rock. There was no Plymouth Rock; that story came 120 years later. The good ship then sailed back to England, where she was taken apart and her timber used to build a barn.

ken
WEBER

Bummers Come in Threes

When Dale Dunn opened the door to her husband's office, he barely glanced at her. Dale and Mike had been running Dunn & Dunn Insurance together for so long now they could interpret each other's movements without exchanging a word. In this particular instance, Dale knew that Mike would read the visit as "errand; no talk necessary." He would know she'd come in to pick up a file, or leave something, or look after a detail that, for whatever reason, couldn't be done in her own office.

She'd also finished with the morning paper, apparently, for she set it quietly on his desk on her way to the filing cabinet. The headline got his attention immediately.

"Rest of Cuban Sugar Industry Scooped," it read. A smaller headline over the lead story announced: "Castro Completes Nationalization After Only Two Months in Power."

Mike stared at the paper for a long time before he looked at his wife. She was smiling at him gently.

"Thanks for not saying I told you so," he said.

She shrugged. "Could have been worse. We could have had all our money still sitting with Bowman." Then to show him she truly was not angry, she changed the subject. "You look at the applications yet? The ones that came in this morning?"

"Right here," Mike replied, happy to talk about anything except Cuba and Castro and Bowman Sugar Inc. "I assume you saw them? I kind of like the guy from...where is he from again?" He sifted through the paper on his desk and resurrected a neatly presented résumé. "Yes, New Denmark. He's the only one who put on a title page. Lends a little class, doesn't it?"

He handed the résumé to Dale. It was in a clear acetate folder with the front page reading:

R. David Sloat   Tel. No. QUaker 4 –7124
12 Colonial Street   D.O.B. 31 May 1932
New Denmark, Ontario   Present Employer: Islington Insurance

"Looks organized, doesn't he?" Mike enthused. "At least from the appearance of that. And if we are going to have an office way out in Bolton, we sure need someone who is organized, wouldn't you think? By the way, assuming we hire this guy, you don't think Islington's gonna say we stole him, do you? The last thing I want would be — "

The telephone stopped him short. Mike picked it up on first ring. That was another element of established practice at Dunn and Dunn. At the office, a phone call meant business and it was answered immediately. At home it was always a contest between Mike and Dale to see who would finally answer.

"Dunn and Dunn," Mike's tone had shifted into efficiency mode, but in a second, his face told Dale the call was not a welcome one.

"Mikey boy!" the caller began.

With a curl of distaste on his lips, Mike looked up at Dale and mouthed, "Mac. At the service station." With his free hand he made a revolver sign at his right temple.

Dale shook her head and made a revolver sign at the telephone.

In spite of himself, Mike smiled. "Hello, Mac. There's a whiff of disaster in your voice again. What did you find this time?"

"You been feedin' this car Purina 'stead of Texaco, Mikey? Can't say's I blame yuh, though. Yuh gotta feed a dog *dog* food!" Mac cackled at his lame joke as Mike's heart sank?

"How bad is it?'

"Well, Mikey…," Mac cleared his throat, then both nostrils. "I got yer fuel pump righted up. Leastways the leak's stopped. Jeez, what a dog! I mean — a leaking fuel pump! Mikey, that's downright scary!"

Mike pinched his lips. His nostrils flared as he took a deep breath. "And the transmission?" he asked.

"One thing at a time. One thing at a time." Mac's phone calls were not only bad news most of the time; they took forever too. "The hood's unstuck now. That's the good news. But those buttons. I mean…whoever came up with the idea of making buttons out of a gearshift? And then putting them into the middle of the steering wheel? It's nuts! I gotta take the steering column out. The whole steering column! That's gonna take me another day at least."

Dale reached across her husband's desk and gently patted his hand. It was still in the revolver shape, but now was being pressed on his forehead.

"You still there, Mikey?"

"That's two," Mike said.

"Huh? Two what? What're yuh talkin' about?"

ken
WEBER

"Nothing." Mike sat up straight and shifted the receiver to his other hand. "Mac, listen. Don't do any more with the car until I call you back. I've got to think this over. May be best just to write the thing off."

"Yea, sure, Mikey. But look, I gotta bill yuh for —"

"I know. I know." Mike cut him off. "Of course you do. Just hold off. I'll call you again before, say, one o'clock."

He hung up before Mac replied. Silence hung heavy in the office until Dale asked, "What did you mean by 'That's two'?"

The silence continued for another moment while Mike calmed himself. "Number two," he said with some emphasis, "is that damned Edsel that's making Mac rich. You were right about the Edsel. We never should have bought that car."

Dale didn't say anything.

"One is the sugar, the shares in Bowman Sugar Inc. When that Castro guy took over Cuba a couple of months ago, we should have sold all our shares in Bowman Sugar."

"We sold half," Dale said. "Not a complete loss. Could be worse, so don't beat yourself up. It was my decision, too." She began to speak faster. "And as for the Edsel, you know, it's so bad it might even be a collector's item some day. Maybe we should keep it. But all this still doesn't explain the one and the two."

Mike looked up at her. "Threes, Dale. Bummers come in threes. Now, this morning the Bowman shares are one, the Edsel is two. I just wonder what three is going to be?"

Dale took a breath and started to speak, then checked herself, but not before Mike reacted.

"The third," he said. "There's a third already?"

Dale nodded. "Here." She handed back the acetate folder. "R. David Sloat."

What is a "bummer" about R. David Sloat's résumé?

Solution on page 85

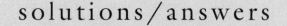

solutions/answers

Solution to "Bummers Come in Threes"

It's not essential to establish the date of this story precisely. A general sense that it is the late 1950s will do. Fidel Castro achieved power in January 1959 and nationalized the sugar industry very quickly. The Ford Motor Company brought out its legendary disaster, the Edsel, for only two years, 1958 and 1959.

In the late 1950s, telephone exchanges in North America had names, not the list of numbers we are accustomed to using today. Thus a number which today might be 928-4567, in 1958-59 would have been WAlnut-8-4567 (or WAverley, or WAterton). (For fans of big band music, Glenn Miller especially, PEnnsylvania 6-5000, if it had been written today, would be 763-5000 — which would make a lousy song title!)

R. David Sloat's telephone exchange would certainly have had a name, but what troubles Dale Dunn is that the name could not possibly have been "Quaker," so this appealing applicant is either a fraud or someone playing a joke. There is no letter Q on a telephone dial. That applies to both old-fashioned rotary telephones and to push-button and cell phones (so being too young to solve this mystery is no excuse!).

Incidentally, although the gear selector on the Edsel was a set of push buttons instead of a lever, this design was not a Ford-alone novelty. Chrysler also did this in the 1950s. Edsel, however, was unique at the time in placing the buttons in the center of the steering wheel.

Answers to "Gimme a T !"

1. Tiberius 2. TNT 3. Steve Allen and then Jack Paar 4 A teetotaler eschews all forms of alcoholic drink. A teetotum is a small top that can be spun with the fingers. 5. Tug of War. Its last year was 1920. 6. "all fruits" 7. Kermit The Frog 8. Taiwan, Tajikistan (or Tadzhikistan), Tanzania, Thailand, Togo, Tonga, Trinidad and Tobago, Tunisia, Turkey, Turkmenistan, Tuvalu 9. Tony, Oscar, Emmy 10. To a tittle (a precisely positioned printer's mark or pen point) The phrase was around long before T-squares.

Answers to "You Can't Have One..."

1. Arthur Sullivan 2. Mr. Hyde 3. Butch Cassidy was born George Leroy Parker. Sundance was Longbaugh 4. right eye 5. Henry Stanley followed the Congo after "finding" Livingstone (who wasn't lost). 6. Seigfried. His co-magician appears with black hair (usually). 7. Oliver Hardy was born near Atlanta, GA. Stan Laurel was born in England 8. Phil Esposito was a forward (center); Tony played goal. 9. Charles Mason was an astronomer; with his assistant, Jeremiah Dixon, he unintentionally divided the U.S. into North and South. 10. Dale. Chip has a black nose. 11. Tommy Smothers played the bass and was the straight man. Dick Smothers did the joking. 12. Dear Ann of Ann Landers is Esther Pauline. Pauline Esther is Dear Abby. (Twins born July 4, 1918.)

Answers to "Longest Unguarded Border"

1. Nova Scotia, Prince Edward Island, and Newfoundland 2. (5) Saskatchewan in Canada, and New Mexico, Colorado, Utah, Wyoming in the U.S. 3. In Canada, there are three: Newfoundland, Prince Edward Island, and Nova Scotia. (Quebec is on the Gulf of St. Lawrence, Ungava Bay and

Hudson Strait; New Brunswick's coasts are on the Bay of Fundy, Northumberland Strait, and Gulf of St. Lawrence. In the U.S., there are 13: New Hampshire, Massachusetts, Rhode Island, Connecticut, New York (via Long Island), New Jersey, Delaware, Maryland, Virginia, North & South Carolina, Georgia, Florida. (Maine is on the Gulf of Maine.) 4. Northwest Territories 5. (3) Iowa, Utah, Ohio 6. Alberta (after Princess Alberta Louise, sixth child of Queen Victoria); Georgia, after George II. 7. Quebec touches three other provinces. Tennessee and Missouri touch eight other states. 8 One Canadian province: Ontario; eight states: Minnesota, Wisconsin, Illinois, Indiana, Michigan, Ohio, Pennsylvania, New York. 9. Letter E 10. (25) Canada: BC, AB, MB, NS; United States: AL, AK, AZ, CA, FL, GA, IN, IW, LA, MN, MT, NB, NV, NC, ND, OK, PA, SC, SD, VA, WV.

Answers to "Hands-Free Word Adventure: If you can read this, then you can spell…"

Khrushchev (Nikita Sergeevich, 1894-1971). The name is spelled three different ways in the narrative: Krushchev; Khrushev, Khrushchev.

Answers to "Hands-Free Word Adventure: Oh, no! Not more puns!"

appear: member of the House of Lords; brotherhood: the crook in your family; cadence: why Kay always flunks; cantaloupe: can't get engaged either; denounce: parts of speech (like deverbs, etc.); drivel: light rain and mift; eureka: you don't look too good either; gumption: boycott of Dubble Bubble; intense: where campers sleep; misconduct: what you do if you're on page 7 and the orchestra's on page 8; noble: the absolute truth; paraffins: the first thing you see on a '59 De Soto; robbers: worn in Minnesota on wet days; sherbet-hot tip at the track; tithe: thtrings around garbage bagth.

Answers to "Pen-Free Puzzle Posers (Moderate)"

Putting the cubes together

1. (a) 27 (b) 6 (c) 36   2. (a) 12 (b) 6 (c) 1 (d) 8   3. (a) 3 (b) 14 (c) 36 (d) 24

Answers to "Pen-Free Puzzle Posers (Challenge)"

One hunter would straddle another piggyback-style and be carried to a breathing hole. At the hole, the hunter being carried would quietly slide off and stand while the footsteps (the carrying hunter) went on past the hole, creating the impression that it had not been chosen. Usually this carrier hunter would also make noises at any other breathing holes nearby so that the seals would instinctively go to the targeted one.

6 divided by 6 plus 6 equals 7
$6/6 + 6 = 7$

44 divided by 4 equals 11
$44/4 = 11$

9 divided by 9 plus 99 equals 100
$9/9 + 99 = 100$

3 times 3 times 3 minus 3 equals 24
$3 \times 3 \times 3 - 3 = 24$

The bag of diamonds is best calculated in the reverse order of theft. If the third thief left eight and thought he had taken one third (four) the second thief must have left twelve. If the second thief took a third (six) then she had been left eighteen by the first. The first then must have taken a third of twenty-seven. That's how many diamonds were in the sealed bag.

section FOUR

emerge informed

Having forgotten all about the Alamo, Mexican general Santa Anna brought some chicle to American inventor Thomas Adams in 1839. Chicle is a substance derived from the sapodilla tree, and the general had a get-rich scheme: figure out how to use it to make rubber. Adams tried for years but had no luck. He did notice, though, that his employees were always chewing the stuff. Adams Chiclets became a hit at about the same time that Santa Anna died (1876), so the general never got a cent out of the idea. (But he did get to be president of Mexico four different times.)

To get his first-ever completed car out of the shop on June 4, 1896, Henry Ford had to knock out a wall. Understandably, such sloppy forward planning rather annoyed his landlord, but he was later placated when Ford replaced the wall with what was, arguably, the world's first garage door.

Important camel facts: Camel milk does not curdle. Camels do not have a gall bladder. For over a hundred years it has been illegal to ride a camel on the highways of British Columbia. (All the above information is valid for both dromedaries (the one-hump model) and for bactrians (the two-humped variety that is far less common — except in Mongolia, where they are in the majority).

Among the country music titles turned down by Branch Records in its early days was "Get Your Tongue Out of My Mouth, 'Cause I'm Kissin' You Goodbye."

That thing a shoe salesperson uses to measure your feet is called a Brannock Device.

shifts of (movie star) wit

Elsa Lanchester on Maureen O'Hara:

"She looked as if butter wouldn't melt in her mouth — or anywhere else."

Frank Sinatra on Robert Redford:

"Well, at least he has found his true love. What a pity he can't marry himself."

King Vidor on Gary Cooper:

"He got a reputation as a great actor just by thinking hard about the next line."

Walter Matthau to Barbra Streisand:

"I have more talent in my smallest fart than you have in your entire body."

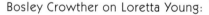

Bosley Crowther on Loretta Young:

"Whatever it is this young actress never had, she still hasn't got it."

Rosanna Arquette on Madonna:

"She jumped right into the movie game — but I think people should learn to act first."

Rodney Dangerfield on Richard Burton:

"Nice guy, but he drinks too much. His last urine sample had an olive in it."

Howard Dietz on Tallulah Bankhead:

"A day away from Tallulah is like a month in the country."

Ava Gardner on Clark Gable:

"Clark is the sort of guy, if you say, 'Clark, how are ya' — he's stuck for an answer."

Marlon Brando on Frank Sinatra:

"He's the kind of guy, in heaven he'll give God a bad time for making him bald."

Richard Winnington on Paul Henreid:

"He looks like his idea of fun is finding a nice cold, damp grave and sitting in it."

Mamie van Doren on Warren Beatty:

"He's in danger of waking up one morning in his own arms."

Bette Davis on Joan Crawford:

"The best time I ever had in Hollywood was when I pushed her down the stairs in *Whatever Happened to Baby Jane?*"

 not their finest hour

Until the 1937 Oscars were actually presented, no one but the Academy Committee knew that Spencer Tracy had won Best Actor. Well, the Academy and a few inside workers — one of whom checked the statuettes and found that the engraver had etched in "Dick Tracy." A repairable error as it turned out.

These too were repairable errors, though nobody bothered...

You may have to rewind your VCR several times, but it's there. During the chariot race in *Ben Hur* (1959), off in the distance there's a little red sports car driving by the Coliseum.

The Sound of Music (1965) is set in the 1930s, in pre-World War II Austria. In one scene, there is a crate of oranges bearing the stamp "Produce of Israel." If nothing else, the purchase is somewhat prescient of the Von Trapps, since Israel did not become a country until 1948.

Billy Wilder's film noir *Double Indemnity* (1944) casts Fred MacMurray as a good-timing, high-living bachelor. An unlikely role for Fred, whose personal life was known to be stable. At the time of filming, Fred was married to his long-time first wife, Lillian Lamont, and throughout the movie he can be seen wearing his wedding band.

Sir Alec Guinness won just about every critical award in filmdom, including the Oscar for Best Actor for his performance in *The Bridge on the River Kwai* (1957). But that still wasn't enough to get his name spelled right in the movie's credits.

Since not many war movies make sense to begin with, it should not be surprising that for a lingering dramatic shot of the setting sun in *The Green Berets* (1968) the camera is pointing east.

Even the great Mahatama's peasants can't be trusted. In *Gandhi* (1982), one of them following the man of peace to the Ganges is wearing Adidas tennis shoes.

Raymond Massey is still regarded as giving the best portrayal, bar none, of Abraham Lincoln. He must have impressed everyone on the set as well as in the theater, for on the soundtrack of *Abe Lincoln in Illinois* (1940) a crowd of well-wishers shouts "Good-bye, Mr. Lincoln!" Except for one who yells, "Good-bye, Mr. Massey!"

Cleopatra had a budget of $43 million — in 1963! Yet during a very elaborate bath scene, a sponge, obviously plastic, floats by Elizabeth Taylor. A close look reinforces the impression that it must have cost at least 25¢.

trivia test

Season's Greetings From Rollo the Red-Nosed Reindeer

When Montgomery Ward stores asked copywriter Robert May to develop a Christmas promotion for 1939, they had no idea he'd come up with the most popular commercial character since Santa Claus. What the executives did know, however, was that they didn't like the name May chose for his reindeer with the red nose. "Rollo," they said, just won't do. May returned to the drawing board and came back with "Randolph." "Even worse!" the execs lamented. Fortunately, May's four-year-old daughter was his backup consultant. It was she who suggested "Rudolph."

1. Clement Moore's famous poem established the idea that old St. Nick lands his sleigh and eight reindeer on the roof and then comes down the chimney with presents. What's the title of that poem?

2. The best known of the sacred Christmas carols, "Silent Night," was accompanied on a guitar at its first public performance. In what country?

3. Wenceslas went out with his page (when the snow lay round about) on the Feast of Stephen. When is the Feast of Stephen?

4. "Serenade in Blue" was not even nominated for the Best Song Oscar in 1942. But "Pig Foot Pete" was, along with "There's a Breeze on Lake Louise," and "White Christmas." "White Christmas" won. From what movie?

5. A sprig of mistletoe over a doorway is supposed to cause some kissing. What ancient priests taught that mistletoe had special powers? (It's also thought these priests built what we now call Stonehenge.)

6. Everyone knows the title of the Christmas oratorio by Handel that made its debut in 1742. In what city was the debut performance?

7. Chances are you may have been "wassailing" at some time over the Christmas seasons past. What does "wassail" mean?

ken
WEBER

8. Some knights heard Henry II of England wish he could be rid of this "damned priest," so they murdered the priest on Christmas Day, in 1170. Who was the priest?

9. According to Charles Dickens, in *A Christmas Carol*, Scrooge thought Christmas was "humbug" until a few ghosts straightened him out. What is Scrooge's first name?

10. What conifer holds top position as the most popular "Christmas tree"?

Answers on page 114

this could take a minute, so be sure there's no one waiting

The Mays and Musts of the Limerick

First, take the test.

> 'Tis said of a lady named Lear
> Who admits to a fondness for beer —
> Her resistance diminishes
> With each one she finishes.
> (Now any last line will do here.)

The "last line" that comes to mind as you read this little narrative of the lady named Lear is probably the best indicator of how you view the limerick. If it is a suggestive line — or lusty or ribald — you're in popular company, for it's a widely held perception that limericks are bawdy, plain and simple.

Granted, many are. In fact it's probably safe to say that the best known and most frequently recited ones fall into that category. Take, for example, the opening line, "There was an old man from Nantucket." It's rare to find an English-speaking adult male who does not, on hearing it, chuckle, or shake his head, possibly nod in embarrassment, or respond with a lascivious grin. "Nantucket" is infamous as a locker room rite-of-passage and ranks as an enduring all-star in the blue leagues. At the same time, it demonstrates a very crucial point about the limerick genre. Although it is easy to remember (memorability is a limerick "must") "Nantucket" — the raunchy version — is only mildly witty at best. More important, it's missing a basic limerick essential: the truly clever last-line twist. Ironically, the original version, the one on which the debauched rendition is based, is almost forgotten. Yet it's a classic example of how a limerick is supposed to work. It first appeared in the *Princeton Tiger* over a century ago:

> There was an old man from Nantucket,
> Who kept all his cash in a bucket.
> His daughter, named Nan,
> Ran away with a man —
> And as for the bucket, Nantucket!

As though to reinforce the fact that to be clever is really the whole point of a limerick, the *Chicago Tribune* then published this sequel:

> Pa followed the pair to Pawtucket
> (The man and the girl with the bucket)
> Where he said to the man,
> "You're welcome to Nan,"
> But as for the bucket, Pawtucket.

Not to be outdone, the *New York Press* appended yet another twist:

> Then the pair followed Pa to Manhasset,
> Where he still held the cash as an asset.
> But Nan and the man
> Stole the money and ran.
> And as for the bucket, Manhasset.

If nothing else, such repartee demonstrates that to be successful, a limerick requires something cerebrally special: a twist, a surprise, a delicious double entendre or play on words. Even if it's a bit salacious or more than a bit lewd, if it's sufficiently clever, a limerick is not only poetic, but also socially acceptable. To whit:

A geologist digging at Gnossal
Uncovered a fossil colossal.
He could tell by the bend
And the shape of the end,
'Twas the peter of Paul the Apostle.

or

A German musician named Bäger,
Spurred on by a very high wager,
Proceeded to fart
The complete oboe part
Of Haydn's octet in A major.

or

There was a young girl who begat
Three babies named Matt, Pat and Tat.
It was fun in the breeding
But hell in the feeding
When she found there was no tit for Tat!

Still, given the vast number of successful limericks that lean toward sex or body parts (usually both!) it is tempting to agree with the following limerical observation.

A limerick packs laughs anatomical
Into space that is most economical.
But the good ones I've seen
So rarely are clean,
And the clean ones so rarely are comical.

Yet aficionados of the form are encouraged by the number that succeed admirably (as in the Nantucket sequence) with nary a mention of anatomy or its possible application in unsanctioned endeavors. Ogden Nash was one who led the way:

There was a fellow named Fonda
Who was squeezed by a large anaconda.
Now he's only a smear
With part of him here,
And the rest of him somewhere out yonda.

Oliver Wendell Holmes (père) got into the act too — also most respectably:

> The Reverend Henry Ward Beecher
> Called a hen a most elegant creature.
> The hen, pleased with that,
> Laid an egg in his hat,
> And thus did the hen reward Beecher.

Interestingly, when this Holmes piece was written (around 1870), the genre was in the middle of a very restricted period in its development. Although the form can supposedly be traced as far back as 400 B.C., when Aristophanes ended his play *The Wasps* with a limerick-like song (another school of thought has it that Irish mercenaries from Limerick brought it back from France, where they'd hired out in the eighteenth century) most devotees grant the lion's share of credit to English writer Edward Lear. In 1846 Lear published his *Book of Nonsense,* a volume filled with limericks that unquestionably were responsible for placing this type of poetry front and center in the public consciousness. However, while Lear's limericks may have titillated his contemporaries, they are pretty dull by our standards. It's not that they are so tame compared to what we know today (although they are), but what Lear's efforts lack, much of the time, is that all-important clever last-line twist. He tended to simply end his poems by repeating the first line, or repeating it with a slight modification, almost as if he'd run out of creative steam after line four. For example:

> There was an old man of Quebec,
> A beetle ran over his neck;
> But he cried, "With a needle
> I'll slay you, O beadle!"*
> That angry old man of Quebec.

Because most limerick writers of his day then followed the standard Lear established, the repeated last line, or slightly altered last line became the dominant model. Fortunately for the future of the form, some writers, like Holmes above and an anonymous contemporary here, were able to rise above the occasion splendidly:

---

*Lear's contemporaries would have enjoyed this pun. "Beadles" were English church officials who kept order, ushered, etc., and had a reputation for being pompous.

ken
WEBER

A certain young chap Bill B. Beebee
Was engaged to a lady named Phoebe.
"But," said he, "I must see
Re the clergyman's fee,
Before Phoebe be Phoebe B. Beebee!"

But these are exceptions. Most early emulators of the Lear standard, in our terms, fell disastrously short. Even established authors had trouble. Nobel Prize winner Rudyard Kipling comes close with this one, especially with the language liberties he takes in lines 3 and 4, but his Lear-like and rather unwitty repetition of "Quebec" reduces the ultimate impact.

There was a young man of Quebec
Who was buried in snow to his neck.
When asked, "Are you frizz?"
He replied, "Yes I is.
But we don't call this cold in Quebec."

Ironically, it may have been the shift toward bawdiness that helped carve out a secure place for the limerick in the literary canon. At first, the subjects of a limerick, the principal characters, tended to be young men, or more frequently old men, and most of these tended to engage in rather addlepated behavior. But as time passed, these unspecified old men (and their younger counterparts) gradually became more precisely identified, sometimes by name, more often by profession, most frequently, it seems, lascivious members of the clergy. In any case, by the early twentieth century, bishops, curates, vicars, and priests* were being lined up with young ladies (most often together, and in the prone position) to liberate (some would say excessively) the genre.

Variety of subject soon became a widely accepted "may" for the limerick, Lear's precedent notwithstanding, so that by the early twentieth century, the old men, young men, clergy, and young ladies were joined by every conceivable subject, from wrestlers to gauchos to presidents.

---

*The Church of England seems to command by far the lion's share of clergy-based limericks, with the pope of Rome a very distant second. (Here followeth a mild sample.)
A dainty young lady from Devon
Was attacked in a thicket by seven
Anglican priests —
Libidinous beasts —
Of such is the kingdom of heaven.

Curiously, given that the writing and recitation of limericks tends to have a very pronounced male gender connection, there are very few limericks about sports, the following being a notable exception.

> A team playing baseball in Dallas
> Called the umpire a "shit" out of malice,
> While this worthy had fits
> The team made eight hits,
> And a girl in the bleachers named Alice.

On the other hand, music, musicians, and especially classical composers, come in for a generous share.

> A lady musician named Tharp
> Got her bust tangled up in her harp.
> When protest arose,
> She was forced to transpose
> Bach's G-minor Suite to C sharp.

Tharp, the lady musician above, illustrates an interesting may/must feature of the limerick. Clearly, hers is a deliberately concocted name, something limerick writers "may" do, and do so freely in order to meet an absolute "must": that lines 1-2-5, and lines 3-4 must rhyme. Although the majority of writers therefore start with proper nouns, and strive for very easy-to-rhyme place names (which explains the tempting frequency of Khartoum, Ghent, Bombay, Spain) or surnames like Astor, Flynn, McNair, it is quite permissible to lead off with the entirely unusual, too. Words like "revanche" (rhymes with Blanche and ranch) or even phrases (for example, "I am" rhymes with Siam and Khayyam) are worked in deftly. In fact, the clever twist factor is sometimes more readily achieved when the writer stays away from proper noun rhymes altogether.

> She wasn't what one would call pretty,
> And other girls offered her pity.
> So nobody guessed
> That her Wasserman test
> Involved half of the men in the city!

Along with rhyme, another absolute must of the limerick form is proper rhythm. The two features, of course, are what make examples of the genre so easy to remember and recite. In a perfectly structured limerick, lines 1, 2 and 5 begin with an iambic "foot" (da DUM) followed by two anapestes (da da DUM, da da DUM), as in the following:

> A BEAU-ti-ful MAI-den named KATE
> Re-CLINED in the DARK with her MATE
>
> _____
>
> _____
>
> But O-ther-wise DO-ing first RATE.

Lines 3 and 4, the shorter ones, have one iamb and one anapest:

> When ASKED how she FARED
> She SAID she was SCARED

The two requirements, exact rhythm and rhyme, are rigorously applied, for they are what distinguish the form so clearly from other short verse. Yet, such is the wit of limerick writers that even restrictions offer opportunity:

> There was a young man of Japan
> Who wrote verses that never would scan.
> When they said, "But the thing
> Doesn't go with a swing."
> He said, "Yes, I always try to get as many words into the last line as I possibly can."

or

> There was a young man from France
> Who waited ten years for his chance.
> Then he muffed it.

Fortunately for limerick lovers, the rhythm rules (more so than those governing rhyme) bend with reasonable ease. Each of lines 3 and 4 below, for example, have an extra syllable that not only enhances the appeal of the verse but also pose no difficulty whatever to a recitation:

> There was a young sailor named Gates
> Who got along well with his mates
> Till he fell on a cutlass
> Which rendered him buttless
> And practically useless on dates.

The ultimate achievement for any limerick scholar is to pen a truly memorable example of the species. No mean task, especially if all the "musts" are to be met. If you are going to try, veterans advise writing the fifth line first, and then working backward to lines 1 and 2 to establish the subject and the scene. The middle lines further the situation and are often what lifts a limerick to elegance, so they should not be treated lightly. Above all, the leading practitioners say, never stop polishing and re-polishing your results. At the very least, the extent of your endeavor should match that of the anonymous wordsmith who described the process thusly:

> You labor from midnight to morn
> Consuming a gallon of corn.
> Tho' you pass out completely,
> The last line comes neatly,
> For thus is a limerick born.

emerge informed

There are only two Triple Continental Divides in the world. One is in the Canadian Rockies. Here, the Columbia River flows down the west side to the Pacific; the Athabasca River flows down the north side to the Arctic, and the North Saskatchewan River flows east to the Atlantic via Hudson Bay. The other Triple Divide is in Siberia.

A jeroboam (of champagne) holds about 104 ounces, twice the capacity of a magnum, while a nebuchadnezzar holds 520. A hogshead (of wine) can hold anywhere from 62.5 to 140 gallons, though in the U.S. a hogshead is rated for 63. It's pronounced HOGZ' hed, by the way, and has nothing to do with headcheese, a jellied loaf which, in upscale form, is made of hog brains. Makers of downmarket headcheese usually toss in the hog's tongue and feet — chopped up, of course.

Who is the greatest boxer of all time? Aficionados agree no one has yet come close to either Rocky Marciano (born Rocco Marchegiano) or Muhammed Ali (born Cassius Clay). In 1969 a computerized bout between the two had Marciano winning by a knockout in the thirteenth round. In a similar computerization in England the same year, Ali won.

Alfred Hitchcock had no belly button, a fact confirmed by actress Karen Black on the source of all wisdom and truth in the 1980s, *The Joan Rivers Show*. Hitchcock's little connecting valve had been removed during surgery, and Black said Hitchcock told her this while showing her his stomach. (A commercial break interrupted any further exposures.)

Napoleon was known to have ailurophobia, the irrational fear of cats. He also had hemorrhoids, though it's difficult to see a connection. Because he was short, Napoleon customarily sat on his great horse Marengo to observe the progress of a battle. At Waterloo, according to his officers' accounts, he did not use his accustomed perch with any regularity, forcing the speculation that the outcome of one of history's greatest battles may have been predestined by the Emperor's sore derriere.

hands-free
word adventure

The game's the thing

OK, you're on first and the chips are down. First offering's a slider and the batter takes. If you don't steal, you could end up behind the eight ball. But if you take the plunge and fail, who takes the fall, you or the first base coach? Traditionally, you know you're not supposed to take the bull by the horns. Your task is to knuckle down and hold the line until the coach says to shoot for second. If you become a cropper, well, the ball's in his court because he calls the shots. Let him be the pigeon.

Still, it's only the first pitch. No way you'll put the game in the gutter if you're not out of the blocks this time. Besides, you love to feint. So tease him. Jab your fingers into the dirt and pick some up. You know the drill. Let it dribble out slowly, lean toward second. Be a bird, be a butterfly, see if he'll take the bait and throw. Remember, he's the one in a box. Make it as rough as you can.

How many different sports and games can you find in the paragraph above? Baseball, obviously, is all over the place (on first, slider, batter). Poker is in there too (the chips). There are at least twenty-eight more. Some words do multiple duty.

Answers on page 114

 # shifts of (movie review) wit

When movie critic Anthony Lane made this comment about *The Scarlet Letter*, he was indulging in the long-established tradition of leading with a stinger: "Roland Joffe's film is, in the words of the opening credits, 'freely adapted from the novel by Nathaniel Hawthorne' — in the same way that methane is freely adapted from cows."

Movie reviews have been shifting wit for over a hundred years now, though earlier ones may not have been quite as clever as Lane's. The June 15, 1896, issue of *Chap Book* merely offered "absolutely disgusting" as its opinion of *The Kiss*, the first-ever movie to fulfill the promise of its title. But Lane's "methane" jab was by no means the first odorous review. Way back in 1687, William Winstanley could hardly wait until poet John Milton's body was cold before writing: "His fame has gone out like a candle and his memory will always stink."

And, by the use of metaphor, both Lane and Winstanley reveal themselves as participants of yet another tradition. Among some of their peers are Nicolai Sloviev, who reviewed the premiere of Tchaikovsky's First Piano Concerto in 1871: "like the first pancake, a flop." And art critic John Ruskin, who saw Beethoven's symphonies this way, in 1881: "like the upsetting of bags of nails, with here and there a dropped hammer."

Still, for out and out, slamdunk bitchiness, nothing beats today's critics of the cinema. Cases in point...

Christopher Tookey in the London *Sunday Telegraph,* on *Desperate Hours* (1991): "one of those films which should never have been released, even on parole. It's a danger to itself."

John Simon on *Camelot* (1967): "roughly comparable to reading a three-volume novel in a language of which one knows only the alphabet."

Judy Griel on *Beyond the Wall* (1959): "I've seen better film on teeth."

going out in style: odd ends

Until Spain joined the prosperity of the European community, bus travel in that country, even in the cities, was frequently of Third World standard. Such was the case one day in Barcelona, where the only space a bus passenger could find was up on the roof with the freight. No sooner had he scrambled up when a sudden heavy downpour prompted him to seek shelter in an empty coffin. There, he fell asleep until the sound of two new roof-riders talking woke him up. When he raised the lid and asked if it had stopped raining, the two jumped off in terror. One broke his arm and lived to describe the incident. The other landed safely but then had a coronary.

Composer Pietro Guglielmi (1727–1804) wanted to see how high the voice of a brilliant new castrato, Luca Fabbris, could soar, and kept pushing for more and more stratospheric notes until the young boy collapsed and died. Musicologists speculate the cause was an aneurysm. It was about this time, by the way, that Guglielmi turned from opera to sacred music (which, at the time, also made frequent use of castrati).

Of all the low blows directed at bald guys, one of the worst is the alleged demise of the Greek poet and playwright Aeschylus (525–456 B.C.). Several ancient biographies have it that his death came about when an erne (a sea eagle), looking to smash the shell of a tortoise on a rock, dropped it instead on Aeschylus's shiny pate.

Scholar, scientist, logician Francis Bacon seized an opportunity for experimentation while riding in his carriage on a cold spring morning in 1626. He had been thinking about principles of refrigeration, and since his carriage was having difficulty getting through the snow in any case, he had the driver stop at a farm, where he bought a chicken, killed it, and stuffed it with snow. His intent was to compare its rate of putrefaction with that of a no-snow chicken. Unfortunately, he got pneumonia running around in the cold and died soon after the chicken did.

There are those who think it a bit macabre that country music great Hank Williams died in the back seat of a Cadillac in 1955, shortly after he'd recorded "I'll Never Get Out of This World Alive." But that irony pales when compared with that attached to gangster Jack Zuta. He'd run afoul of Al Capone, with the inevitable result. When Capone's hit men caught up with Zuta in a resort hotel near Milwaukee, their fire was so intense it slammed his body into a coin-operated piano, which then began to play "Good for You, Bad for Me."

pen-free puzzle posers
(EASY)

1. Bob needed only a glance at the three playing cards before pressing the speed dial on his cell phone.

"There's a three just to the right of a two," he said to the voice that merely grunted a response at the other end. "And a three just to the left of a three."

Again there was a grunt.

"A spade's just to the left of a heart and — a...de...ri..."

"You're breaking up!" The voice at the other end was emphatic.

"Sorr... ...atteries. And a spade just to the right of a spade. Come through?"

"Yeah, got it."

What are the three playing cards?

2. Correct the equation below. This one is definitely pen-free. Eraser free too.

$$X + I = IX$$

3. The studio assistant waited until all the students had left before she went around and gathered up all the partly finished paintings. Ten of them altogether. At Table A, there were three to put away. It had been a good day all round, she thought. Every student had got a good start, but then that was fairly typical for still lifes. They always went over well. She picked up two at table B and two more at table C. Nobody had given up, as often happened, which meant that tomorrow when this class began, everyone would have something to do, and she could take it easy for a bit. "Yes," the assistant said softly to herself as she gathered the final three paintings from Table D, "a good day."

"A bit of a surprise," she commented later to the art instructor, "an unusual class. There's the three fusspots at D, and those two who won't talk to each other at Table C. Two daughters and two mothers at A. You don't get that every day! And the lovers at B. Some class. Well, they're all working. Who am I to complain?"

The assistant cited eleven people but picked up ten paintings. Why?

Answers on page 114

trivia test

Mysterious Islands

In the Pacific Ocean, about a four-hour jet flight east of Australia, lies Falcon Island. Well, more or less. The island comes and goes. After a hundred years of life as a piece of territory in the British Empire, Falcon Island suddenly disappeared under the waves in 1913. No one fretted much, since it has always been uninhabited (except for a few male blue-footed boobies who used it as a place to pick up girls). However, it suddenly reappeared in 1926, much to the relief of the boobies, only to go under again in 1949. It hasn't been seen since.

1. Match the islands in the left column with a proper description in the right column.

    Easter   (a) issuer of one of the rarest stamps in the world

    Mauritius   (b) site of a giant statue in ancient times

    Rhodes   (c) huge statues still stand there

    Hawaii   (d) largest island in North America

    Baffin   (e) formerly known as Sandwich Islands

2. On what Caribbean island did Christopher Columbus land first, in 1492?

3. The island of Elba and the island of St. Helena: Napoleon was exiled on both. On which one was he exiled first?

4. Excluding Australia, which geographers call a "continent," what is the world's largest island?

5. The *Bounty*'s mutineers sent Captain Bligh and his followers off in a little boat in 1789 and then settled on what island in the Pacific?

6. How many of Canada's ten provinces are islands?

7. What "bird" island group is named after wild dogs that sailors found there?

8. What island country claims 100 percent adult literacy?

9. In what body of water are there two "dairy cow" islands?

10. True or false: Bermuda is an island in the Caribbean Sea.

Answers on page 114

emerge informed

Things could be worse. You could be an editor with Swedish publisher Almqvist & Lundström, whose publications include *Bead Making in Scandinavia in the Early Middle Ages* (1976); *The Music of the Mongols* (1943); and *Lappish Bear Graves in Northern Sweden* (1974). Better to work for Haldeman-Julius. Sample works: *How to Test Your Urine at Home* (1935). Or MacMillan: *On the Conditions Under Which Leprosy Has Declined in Iceland* (1895).

In the original story of Pinocchio, by Carlo Lorenzini (published 1881 under nom de plume C. Collodi), the little puppet is a genuine brat. He tromps Jiminy Cricket with his foot and becomes a career delinquent. The behavior must have appealed to someone out there. The story appeared that way in over 200 languages and dialects before the Disney Studios upgraded Pinocchio's image in 1940.

Other publishing discoveries we have made: A. Chapuis's *The History of the Self-Winding Watch* (Batsford, 1952); Sir Charles Ball's *Ball on the Rectum* (Hodder & Stoughton, 1908); W. Neal's *Searching for Railway Telegraph Insulators* (Signal Box Press, 1982); and C. McSherry's *Sex Instruction for Irish Farmers* (Mercier Press, 1980). These need not be read in the preceding sequence.

"Hangman's wages" are 13 cents (or thirteen pence, ha'penny). Tradition has it the phrase arose because a hangman's fee, one shilling (12 cents) was added to the cost of the rope: 1 cent. Seekers of truth (viz., readers of *The Toilet Papers*) will want to know that James I, to stabilize currency at the beginning of the seventeenth century, declared the Scottish mark to be worth 13 pence. Hangmen in Scotland were traditionally paid one mark per drop, and that is how the phrase came about.

In comedian Eddie Murphy's two concert movies, *Delirious* (1983) and *Raw* (1987), he expletes a total of 921 times, for an average of one expletive every 14.5 seconds. The total includes 16 uses of the "n" word, which, like a particular "f" word, once used to mean "a bundle of sticks or twigs," and has only recently been added to the compendium of scurrility frowned upon by the MPPA (Motion Picture Producers of America).

for deposit in your "one-up" account

It is your duty to correct the misinformed

In the fifty-six short stories and four novels by Arthur Conan Doyle, Sherlock Holmes never once said, "Elementary, my dear Watson." British actor Basil Rathbone, who became identified with the Holmes character in movies of the 1930s and '40s, made the phrase famous.

$$\$\$$$

James Cagney never said, "You dirty rat!" in any of his 70-plus movies. Nor did Charles Boyer ever say, "Come with me to the Casbah" in any of his movies (and most especially not in *Algiers,* the 1938 movie in which he plays Pepe, a crook who lives in the Casbah). Boyer said the phrase was a fabrication of his press agent. Cagney simply said that, in his case, it just never happened.

$$\$\$$$

ken
WEBER

The Bible does not say, "Spare the rod and spoil the child." English poet Samuel Butler wrote, "Then spare the rod and spoil the child" in *Hudibras* (1664). The Bible does say, "He that spareth his rod hateth his son" in Proverbs 13:24. The Bible also does not say, "Cleanliness is next to Godliness." That is from the founder of Methodism, John Wesley, in one of his published sermons ("On Dress"). Wesley lifted it, without credit, from second-century Hebrew sage Phineas ben-Yair.

$$\$\$$$

W. C. Fields never said, "Anybody who hates children and dogs can't be all bad." It was writer Leo Rosten, who said it about Fields, and what he said was, "Anybody who hates dogs and babies can't be all bad."

$$\$\$$$

Mark Twain never said, "There are three kinds of lies: lies, damn lies, and statistics." What Twain did, in his autobiography, was quote British prime minister Benjamin Disraeli. And he gives Disraeli the proper credit!

$$\$\$$$

William Maguire never said, "Praise the Lord and pass the ammunition!" during the attack on Pearl Harbor on December 7, 1941. Maguire, a U.S. Navy chaplain, not only denied saying it, he added that even if he had said it, no one would have heard him in the din of battle, anyway. But that didn't stop Frank Loesser from turning it into a hit song in World War II. The phrase, incidentally, was already a slogan in the American Civil War.

$$\$\$$$

Movie producer Sam Goldwyn never said, "I was on the brink of a great abscess." Nor did he ever say, "You've got to take the bull by the teeth," or "Our comedies are not to be laughed at," or even, "A verbal contract isn't worth the paper it's written on." The "abscess" and the "teeth" quips were traced to his staff. The "comedies" quip is a Hollywood one-liner that predates Goldwyn, and what he really said about executive Joseph Schenck was, "His verbal contract is worth more than the paper it's written on."

hands-free
word adventure

Sure you think you know these! So fill in the blanks.
(If you get more than three correct, you are unusually good!)

1   (John Heywood) "Went in _____ ear and out _____."

2.   (Isaac Watts) "Ask me no questions and I'll tell you no _____."

3.   (William Shakespeare) "To _____ the lily."

4.   (Traditional wedding vow) "Till death _____ part."

5.   (Nathan Hale) "I only regret that I have but one life to _____ for my country."

6.   (Proverbs) "Pride goeth before _____."

7.   (I Timothy) "_____ is the root of all evil."

8.   (Vince Lombardi) "Winning isn't everything, _____ _____."

9.   (Walter Colton) "Imitation is the sincerest _____."

10.   (William Shakespeare) "Alas, poor Yorick. I knew him _____."

11.   (Job) "_____ the skin of my teeth."

12.   (Robert Burton) "Birds of a feather _____ together."

Answers on page 114

109

ken
WEBER

pen-free puzzle posers
(MODERATE)

1. Eloise had a reputation for claiming relatives. To her acquaintances, it seemed she was related to just about everyone in the world. None of them were surprised, therefore, when she stopped at a portrait in the local museum one day and announced, "That man, the man in the painting?" Several of the group groaned audibly, but Eloise carried on blithely, "His mother was my mother's mother-in-law!"

No one in the group with Eloise wanted to admit they were remotely interested, for doing so would only encourage her to find more relatives, but the way she had described this situation was too intriguing to ignore, and gradually, all of them figured it out in spite of themselves.

Assuming Eloise is telling the truth, what is her relationship to the man in the portrait?

2. Janet and Peter have not enjoyed a game of golf as much as this one for quite some time now. Conditions are perfect. The weather is beautiful, but the course is not even a bit busy. Lots of time to think about each shot. The kids are at home in good hands. Grandma and Grandpa are babysitting for the weekend. And both of them are right on their game. By the sixth hole, they are tied at nine over par. By the eleventh hole they are tied at seven over par. For the next five holes, the lead see-saws back and forth, but never by more than a single stroke.

Then, at the seventeenth green, a par four, a problem develops. Peter drops his third shot close to the pin, but it rolls into a paper bag that blew onto the green just as he shot. Because the game has taken on serious overtones by now, Janet insists he follow the club rules, which means it will cost him a stroke if he takes the ball out of the paper bag. Peter solved the problem, though, without costing himself a stroke. *How?*

3. Imagine three vertical parallel lines half an inch apart.

Now imagine these three lines being crossed by three horizontal parallel lines. *How many squares have been formed?*

Answers on page 114

trivia test

Dreaming in Color

Only one week after its release in 1958, Sheb Wooley's "One-Eyed, One-Horned, Flying Purple People Eater" became the number one song in North America.

1. What color would you get if you mixed the Beatles' submarine with Thomas Gainsborough's famous painting of a little boy?

2. The Green Lantern is reduced to ordinary mortal strength in the face of this color (also the color of Dick Tracy's raincoat).

3. Phyllis Diller, the Kingston Trio, and several others made their debut at this "Onion" nightclub in the 1950s.

4. This comic book cowboy hero had a small companion who reinforced the former's alleged intelligence by saying, "You betchum, R— R—!"

5. Name the diamond that gets Inspector Clouseau into trouble.

6. What Canadian pilot shot down Manfred von Richthofen (the Red Baron) on April 21, 1918?

7. On what show did Mister Greenjeans make regular appearances?

8. The Lancasters and the Yorks took on each other in the War of the Roses. Which side sported a white rose?

9. The biggest song of 1941 has what two colors in the first line?

10. Each of these authors wrote a book with a color in the title. I've added a clue here to help (or possibly mislead). For example, Anna Sewell's "attractive filly" would be Black Beauty.

    (a) Anton Chekhov's grove (b) Nathaniel Hawthorne's epistle
    (c) Thomas Costain's cup (d) Stephen Crane's decoration (e) Jack London's teeth (f) John Howard Griffin's simile

Answers on page 114

ken
WEBER

more shifts of (movie review) wit

Variety on *Stay Tuned* (1992):

"A picture with nothing for everybody."

Variety on *Lonesome Cowboy* (1970):

"…Andy Warhol's best movie yet, which is like saying a three-year-old has graduated from smearing faeces on the wall to the occasional use of finger paints."

New York Daily News on *Hawk of Powder River* (1948):

"Eddie Dean's latest is in black and white rather than color, but the improvement is hardly noticeable; you can still see him."

Variety on *The Hollywood Knights* (1980):

"…seems determined to set the Guinness Book record for the most grossouts ever packed into one picture."

London Evening Standard on *Buffy the Vampire Slayer* (1992):

"To enjoy this moronic rubbish, you'd need to put your IQ into total unconsciousness."

Pauline Kael, acknowledged as one of the truly great film critics, was fired from *McCall's Magazine* for her review of *The Sound of Music* (1965). Among other less-than-complimentary comments, Kael had this to say:

"…will probably be the most repressive influence on artistic freedom in movies for the next few years." (One can only wonder what actor Christopher Plummer thought of this review, for after the filming of *The Sound of Music* was finished, his comment on co-star Julie Andrews was that "working with her is like being hit on the head with a Valentine card.")

Screenwriter Robert Towne was so upset with the changes made to his script for *Greystoke: The Legend of Tarzan* (1984) that in the credits he had his name replaced with the name of his sheepdog, whom he called P. H. Vasak. (The dog got an Oscar nomination!)

emerge informed

A contemporary of Shakespeare, the playwright Ben Jonson, once told King Charles I, jokingly, that he'd like a square foot of Westminster Abbey. Jonson (1573?-1637) is buried upright in "Poet's Corner" of the Abbey, in a space of about one square foot, which shows that His Majesty had a sense of humor. (Or that perhaps he didn't.)

A surprising number of accounts claim that the first rapid-transit subway is the "Inter-borough," opening in 1904 and running under Manhattan from the Brooklyn Bridge to 145th Street. Not so. The very first underground line, steam-powered, opened in London in 1868. By 1870 the same city had an electrified line. Glasgow, Scotland, opened an electrical line in 1891.

Big league pitcher Hugh Daley (aka Daily) won 74 games between 1882 and 1887, including a no-hitter, and during his short career set a long-standing record of 19 strikeouts in one game. Not bad for a guy with just one arm! But Daley had an advantage after 1884. That was the year the major leagues first allowed pitchers to throw overhand. At the time, the distance from mound to plate was only 50 feet! It didn't become 60 feet 6 inches until 1893. (And if you think the batters had a hard time, consider the catchers. They played barehanded!)

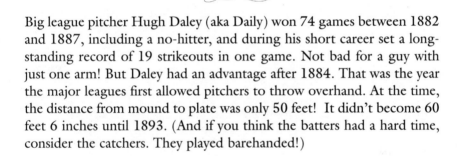

A flock of geese is a gaggle. But once a gaggle is in the air, it becomes a skein. A collective of papillae, on the other hand (or on the arm or neck), is called goose bumps whether the human sporting them is aground or aloft. Use this information while you can, though, for collectives evolve. Today, we know covey as the collective for quail or partridge. *The Dictionary of the Vulgar Tongue,* from 1811, tells us a covey is "a collection of whores."

solutions/answers

Answers to "Season's Greetings from Rollo"

1. "A Visit From Saint Nicholas" is the title of the poem; "'Twas the night before Christmas" is the first line. 2. Austria (A guitar was used because mice had damaged the bellows on the church organ in Oberndorf.) 3. December 26. (Wenceslas was actually a duke, in Bohemia. He was murdered by his brother, the king, about 935.) 4. *Holiday Inn* (Paramount). "Pig Foot Pete" was from *Hellzapoppin* (Universal) and "Lake Louise" from *The Mayor of 44th Street* (RKO) 5. The Druids of ancient Britain and Gaul 6. Dublin (in April, too, not December!) 7. "Wassail" is a toast meaning "good health, good cheer." 8. Thomas à Becket 9. Ebenezer 10. white spruce

Answers to "Mysterious Islands"

1. Easter (c) Mauritius (a) Rhodes (b) Hawaii (e) Baffin (d) 2. San Salvador 3. Elba 4. Greenland 5. Pitcairn 6. Two: Prince Edward Island and Newfoundland 7. Canary Island (after *canis*, for dog) 8. Iceland 9. English Channel (Jersey and Guernsey) 10. False: It is in the Atlantic.

Answers to "Hands-Free Word Adventure: The game's the thing"

pool (eight ball, call the shots); diving (take the plunge); wrestling (the fall); bullfighting (bull by the horns); marbles (knuckle down); football (hold the line); hockey, basketball, archery, rifle shooting (shoot); horse racing, riding (become a cropper); tennis (ball's in his court); skeet shooting (pigeon); soccer, cricket, croquet (pitch); bowling (in the gutter); track and field (out of the blocks); fencing (feint); boxing (jab); gymnastics (drill); basketball (dribble); badminton (bird); swimming (butterfly); fishing (take the bait); lacrosse (box); golf (rough).

Answers to "Dreaming in Color"

1. Yellow Submarine + Blue Boy = green 2. Yellow 3. The Purple Onion 4. Red Ryder 5. The Pink Panther 6. Roy Brown 7. Captain Kangaroo 8. York was a white rose; Lancaster, red. 9. "There'll be blue birds over the white cliffs of Dover" 10. (a) *The Cherry Orchard* (b) *The Scarlet Letter* (c) *The Silver Chalice* (d) *The Red Badge of Courage* (e) *White Fang* (f) *Black Like Me*

Answers to "Hands-Free Word Adventure: Sure you know these!"

1. at the one…at the other 2. fibs 3. paint 4. us do 5. lose 6. Destruction 7. the love of money 8. but wanting to win is 9. of flattery 10. Horatio 11. with 12. will gather

Answers to "Pen-Free Puzzle Posers (Easy)"

The three playing cards from left to right are the 2 of spades, the 3 of spades, and the 5 of hearts.

Turn *The Toilet Papers* upside down and the equation will read XI = I + X

In the art class, there are two mothers and two daughters at Table A. That's three people: a grandmother, her daughter, and her granddaughter. Thus there are three paintings at Table A, and ten people in the art class.

Answers to "Pen-Free Puzzle Posers (Moderate)"

The man in the portrait is Eloise's father.

Peter burned the bag.

Five squares: four 1/2 inch x 1/2 inch, and one 1 inch x 1 inch.

section FIVE

emerge informed

The "noble" gases (radon, neon, argon and xenon, among other regal emanations) won't have a thing to do with other gases because, not unlike many other aristocratic types, they are inert. (If you're counting, their valence number is zero.)

Between 1938 and 1985, 81 percent of the movies released by studios in Hollywood used the line, "Let's get outta here!"

Did the Corinthians ever write back? It seems they did. In the sections of Paul's letters that are rarely heard in church, it's apparent from both the contents and style of language that they were written in reply to information received. They even contain gossip!

In World War I, 25 British pilots were credited with 30 or more dogfight victories. Ten of these pilots were Canadians. The British secretary of state resolutely failed to acknowledge the fact that the "colonials'" training was far superior. Between 1914 and 1918, more British pilots were killed during training than by the enemy.

The phrase synonymous with the double play in baseball is the Chicago Cubs infield, "Tinker to Evers to Chance." The fact is, compared to the shortstop, second and first combos on other National League teams, the Cubs really weren't that good. Most of the other teams in the league came up with more DPs a season than they did (and at least half of theirs went "Evers to Tinker to Chance"). What made this double-play phrase famous was a poem in the *New York Mail* in July 1910, bemoaning the fact that the Giants always came second to the Cubs. It seems that against the Giants, Tinker, Evers and Chance really did work together, and the poem used their names as a refrain.

115

ken
WEBER

shifts of wit

If a "Like, Really Cool!" hall of fame is ever opened, it will include Alvin Waff of Hampton, Virginia. In 1995 he confused brake pedal and accelerator during a 90-degree right turn, slipped between two parked cars, took out a parking meter, crossed a double sidewalk and smashed right through the front wall of the Hangar Restaurant & Lounge, finally coming to rest against the bar. His first words? "Do you have beer on draft?"

Alongside Waff goes a Master of Trinity College, William Whewell. In 1859 he was escorting Queen Victoria over a bridge on the River Cam, which, at the time, was still used as an open sewer. When the Queen asked him about the many little square pieces of paper floating on the stream, he explained, "Those, Madam, carry notices that the river is not fit for bathing."

When Auguste Renoir was asked just how he managed to achieve such realistic flesh tints and shapely forms in his paintings of nudes, he explained, "I just keep painting till I feel like pinching. Then I know I've got it right."

Charles MacArthur, who rightly deserves more fame than for just being Helen Hayes' husband (he was a successful playwright), once got himself and a drinking buddy tossed out of their seats at one of his wife's performances after a lady next to them complained. As the army of ushers descended, he cried out to his friend, "Quick, Lederer! Put your hand up her skirt! We're getting tossed out anyway!"

While a member of Congress, frontiersman Davy Crockett was one of the paying patrons at a touring animal show in Washington. After remarking on the similarity between a monkey in the display and one of his fellow congressmen, Crockett was embarrassed to find that worthy standing behind him. Only temporarily embarrassed, however, for his next comment was, "I suppose I ought to offer an apology. But I don't know whether it should be to you or the monkey."

If the hall of fame has a section for "It probably isn't true but oh, how we wish it were" stories, then this about Alfred, Lord Tennyson, will have pride of place.

As a young man, Tennyson was bothered by hemorrhoids (true) and visited a proctologist. Treatment was successful and for years he went unbothered. Not until he was one of the most famous men in all England (and had become Lord Tennyson) did a recurrence drive him back to the specialist who'd attended him years before. To the poet's surprise the doctor did not recognize him. Until he bent over, and heard, "Ah, Tennyson!"

not their finest hour

"Four decades of studying the history of warfare has made clear to me that the military mind works equally well on both sides. Perhaps that's God's way of preserving the planet." G. H. Smith, emeritus professor of history, University of Toronto.

In the weeks leading up to the first shot of the Franco-Prussian War (1870–71), insiders in the French military were beside themselves over the potential of a radically new and powerful gun, the Mitrailleuse, a rapid-fire weapon they knew could tip the balance in any engagement. But so rigorously did they enforce the need-to-know secrecy about it that the first shipment of guns arrived at the front with no instructions on how to load and fire. Since the Mitrailleuse guns were like nothing they'd ever seen before, and given that there were other things to do now that the shooting had started, the front-line officers simply put them in storage.

ken
WEBER

At an analysis meeting in October 1939, following the invasion of Poland, one topic discussed by the German general staff was the high failure rate of horseshoes. Fully 90 percent of the German land forces during that invasion depended on horse-drawn transport.

On May 26, 1941, due west of St. Nazaire in the Atlantic, the mighty German battleship *Bismarck* was finally located by the Royal Navy — thanks to the Luftwaffe. Chief of staff Hans Jeschonnek had ordered a lengthy radio message sent to the ship to see how his son was doing. Before long, *Bismarck* was being shadowed by the British cruiser HMS *Sheffield*, while the carrier HMS *Ark Royal* and other warships hurried to catch up. To help matters, the *Ark Royal* launched ten torpedo planes in the hopes a hit might at least slow *Bismarck* down. All ten planes dropped their torpedoes on target but all ten torpedoes misfired. Just as well, for it turned out they had attacked HMS *Sheffield!*

"They couldn't hit an elephant at this dist..." Last words of John Joseph Sedgewick, Union general at the Battle of Spotsylvania, May 1864.

On June 5, 1813, at the Battle of Stoney Creek, in the War of 1812, the second in command of the invading American forces, General William Winder, became concerned over the whereabouts of his superior, General John Chandler, and left the command tent to go look for him. Winder got lost, wandered into a British gun emplacement, and was captured. The militia were not trained in professional military niceties, such as proper treatment of a captured field grade officer, so they simply tied him back-to-back with another American officer they'd captured a few minutes before. Chandler.

trivia test

"A horse is a horse, of course, of course."
(Unless it's Mr. Ed.)

Mr. Ed (whose real name was Bamboo Harvester) led the Sunday-night TV ratings for CBS from 1960 to 1965. But Ed would never have made it to the screen if it hadn't been for George Burns and Jack Benny, who bankrolled the producer, Arthur Lubin. Despite Lubin's success with the *Francis the Talking Mule* movies, no other financiers would pay the slightest attention when he brought up his idea of a horse that not only talked, but even got drunk from time to time. Mr. Ed won TV's PATSY Award (for performing animals) in 1962, 1963, 1964 and 1965.

1. What breed of horse was Mr. Ed?

2. According to Shakespeare, which English king ran around Bosworth Field in 1485, crying out, "A horse, a horse! My kingdom for a horse!"

3. Khartoum, well, *part* of a horse named Khartoum, ended up in bed with a Hollywood producer. In what movie?

4. A horse that is "15 hands" is how high? (Hands convert to inches.)

5. How many horses (with riders, of course) on a polo team?

6. Diane Crump finished 15th aboard Fathom in the 1970 Kentucky Derby, thereby coming in not only last but first as well. How come?

7. What English sailor, in a very widely read novel, found himself on a strange island with talking horses known as Houyhnhnms?

8. Match the four real people and the four fictional ones with their horses.

Gene Autry	Black Bess
Mickey Mouse	Buttermilk
Robert E. Lee	Buck
Zorro	Horace Horsecollar
Dick Turpin	Champion
Dudley Do-Right	Tornado
Dale Evans	Traveler
Ben Cartwright	Horse

ken
WEBER

9. According to John Steinbeck, what color was Jody Tiflin's pony?

10. What cockney lady shocked the elegant patrons at the races at Ascot when she urged her favorite to "Move your bloomin' arse!"?

Answers on page 142

this could take a minute, so be sure there's no one waiting

When the Nature of the Human Confronts Human Nature

The Amy Vanderbilt Complete Book of Etiquette offers advice on sneezing, along with advice on swearing and, as you might expect, some thoughts on spitting. It tells you what to do about nervous mannerisms, how to cover up a burp, how to blow your nose at the table, and what to do if you have food caught in your teeth. Amy tells you how to talk to the Pope, what kind of alarm clock to take along in your suitcase, and how to address a letter to a gay couple. But absolutely nowhere in over 900 pages of dense, tiny print, does she tell you what to do if you fart. (It's also a two-way omission, by the way, for not only has she chosen to ignore the farter, she has no advice for the innocent fartee!)

It could be that Amy feels it just isn't done. Or maybe it's just that *she* doesn't. If the latter case were true, it would make her one of the world's tiniest minorities. For if there is a single biological equation common to all human existence, it is this: [eating = farting]. Not only has Amy blithely skipped over this fundamental reality of human existence, she has obviously declined to comment as well on the pair of social equations that follow: [farting = embarrassment] and [farting = giggles].

The biology is relatively simple to understand, if only from experience. A combination of five gases dominates the makeup of a typical decrepitation: nitrogen and oxygen, which you swallow while eating;

and carbon dioxide, hydrogen and methane, which are produced afterward in the large intestine. These gases pay no respect to gender, age, size, profession or class, and are visited indiscriminately upon us all. After that, whether you are a whispering *pffft* type or one of those who can flatten a Douglas fir is a factor of your particular anatomy. But it's not the biology that intrigues. It's the sociology. Why does flatulence stimulate such powerful social reactions?

That a fart can be profoundly embarrassing is a given (though the degree of chagrin may depend somewhat on your social circle; in some groups, a lusty Blue Angel represents a major achievement). The level of embarrassment is also very much driven by where and when the sin is committed. Those elements go a long way toward explaining the behavior of Lord Edward de Vere, 17th Earl of Oxford, in 1580. A prominent courtier in the entourage of Elizabeth I, and a gentleman with a keen sense of his public image, de Vere once drew the worst kind of attention to himself during a low, sweeping bow to the Queen. Although the untimely emission was not without admirers (one of the court chroniclers described it with some awe, as a "mihtee thonderclappe"), his lordship was so embarrassed that he completely withdrew himself from court and did not reappear for a full seven years! Elizabeth's welcome, when he finally mustered the courage to return, is unmatched in the annals of regal obtuseness. "My Lorde," she greeted him, "I hade forgotte the farte."

It takes no great depth of insight to appreciate that odor and noise feature prominently in the depth of humiliation that can accompany a fart. But a prior issue is self-control. Obviously, contemporary arbiters of manners such as Amy Vanderbilt assume you will instinctively manage your anatomy in a pro-social manner when you're in the presence of others. Equally clearly, they assume that you have weighed the shame of an embarrassing release against the pain of retaining it, and come down heavily on the side of the former.

Yet the pain-of-retention side has its champions too. In ancient Rome, the Emperor Claudius once considered passing a decree to permit the breaking of wind at the dinner table, so convinced was he of the possibility that he might die if he didn't let go when he had to. This was early in his reign, however, and before long he discovered that for his own immediate purposes, an edict was unnecessary because his subjects would always go out of their way to imitate the emperor. Farting at the table, therefore, at least during the reign of Claudius, was de rigueur (though it's likely that guests were careful to wait for imperial precedent). An eleventh-century document from the university in Salerno makes no bones about the dangers of suppression. Doctors here advised that holding back elevates the risk of "dropsy, convulsions, vertigo, and frightful colics." In 1585 the essayist Montaigne, better known perhaps for his perceptive essays on the personalities and ideas of his day, also wrote, "God alone knows how many times our bellies, by the refusal of a single fart, have brought us to the door of an agonizing death."

A far less ominous backdrop to the fear of death from farting, not to mention the fear of embarrassment, is the giggle factor. Quite simply, farts make people laugh. Well, maybe not Amy Vanderbilt, but just about everybody else. Look at the number of fart-joke titles on the shelves of your favorite bookstore. Or check the Net for fart-joke exchanges. Even you: If you have continued reading this far, then almost for sure you have several pneumatic jokes in your very own repertoire. You're in good company. Fart jokes — very lengthy and involved fart jokes — have been around for centuries. And none is longer and more involved, as scholars of scatology will hasten to point out, than a best-selling book from 1727, allegedly translated from a Spanish work by "Don Fart-In-Hando, Puffindorft Professor of Bombast at the University of Craccow." The learned Don was none other than noted churchman Jonathan Swift, Dean of St. Patrick's in Dublin.

In the title of this burlesque, Swift manages to intertwine both the giggling and the retention factors, while supposedly holding forth scientifically on the effects of internal gases on women. "The Benefit of Farting Explained," he leads off and then, in typical eighteenth-century style, continues with a lengthy subtitle: "Or, the Fundamental Cause of the Distempers incident to the Fair Sex inquired into, proving 'a posteriori' that most of the Disordures intailed on them are owing to Flatulencies not seasonably vented."

Like most opportunists who take advantage of the laughter that farts seem to stir, Swift chose the medium of print to achieve his ends. Frankly, there was not much else available to him at the time, certainly not the sound effects available to modern practitioners of flatulent foolery such as Mel Brooks in the movies. However, no one thus far in recorded human history has ever duplicated the deliveries of a Frenchman named Josef Pujol, who made his contributions live and on stage. Every night! No treatise on this airy subject could approach completeness without a bow to this utterly fascinating man from Marseilles who, during his vaudeville career from 1887 to 1914, was — quite literally — a farting sensation throughout all of Europe. Pujol was featured across the continent as Le Petomane, which translates literally as "the farter," but in French the word connotes more of a sense of artistry, as in "artistic farter," or perhaps *fartiste*.

As a boy, Pujol discovered that he could take in large quantities of air through the back passage, and that he could not only expel it at will, but also shape the natural audio accompaniment cleverly enough to mimic the different instruments in the woodwind section of a symphony orchestra. A stint in the army provided him with more than ample opportunity to hone his skills in that uniquely male endeavor, the group gross-out, and confirmed the appeal of his talent. As soon as he was mustered out and went to work in the family bakery, he began to put together an act. It was such a thunderous success that by 1892 he was a headliner at the Moulin Rouge, the mecca of the European stage.

Whether it was owing to his natural modesty, or his upbringing, or perhaps to marketing shrewdness, Pujol's virtuosity was always delivered in good taste — good taste, that is, once the nature of the product was discounted. He dressed in a short-tailed red coat and black breeches, and carried white gloves in one hand. He would address the audience, promising them a "performance of petomania," then on hands and knees, and with posterior pointed downstage, he would deliver the opening set. This was a random selection of very carefully controlled eruptions, each delivered in a special context. There were farts from butchers, nuns, generals, grandmothers, and an audience favorite: a little whisper he called "le petite petimide de la jeune fille." He accompanied himself on the trumpet, and dared the audience to identify which was which. The farting miller of Chaucer's *The Canterbury Tales* got a special performance. And he invariably brought the house down with a set of before-and-after comparisons, like "the fart of the bride on the wedding night," a barely audible *wiffut*, followed by "the fart of the bride a week later," a mighty raspberry.

The act lasted about an hour and a half with several short breaks while Pujol went backstage to take in air. Each time he returned with yet another variation. He would be a tailor, and then put out a ten-second rip that sounded precisely like tearing cloth. He would be a soldier, and present different sizes of cannon fire. He would do night scenes with hooting owls and amorous bullfrogs, and ghost scenes with creaking

ken
WEBER

doors. He blew out candles and footlights, and with a tube appropriately placed (inserted off-stage) played tunes on an ocarina. "O Sole Mio" was the most frequently requested. Music was always an important part of the act. With pitch-pipe accuracy, Pujol could fart the tonic note in the key of B major along with the next two notes of the scale. From then on up he would resort to the tube and ocarina. (Musicians with a developed sense of flatulent humor will note the irony in his ability to produce Do, Re, and Me naturally, but not Fa!) One of the popular features in his act that he eventually had to cut back was audience participation. His challenge to a packed house to imitate him, or even to out-fart him, tended to get the audience into such a state that they couldn't settle down. More than once his show closed down early when the audience — always including the cream of Parisian society — had to be evicted.

All this talent made Josef Pujol very rich. At his peak, he was paid three times the fee that the great Sarah Bernhardt got. When Le Petomane was on the playbill, scalpers could name their price. The theaters often had to make special arrangements, too, when Pujol was on. Royalty, Leopold II of Belgium, for one, frequently attended incognito and generated a security fuss. Josef himself was always deadpan, but because the audience was constantly in stitches, the Moulin Rouge hired nurses to patrol the aisles ministering unto women who, according to *Le Figaro,* fainted from hilarity en masse. Their quick revival was important. Not only did they not want to miss anything, but at the end of his performance, Pujol always farted the first line of "La Marseillaise," and the ladies, like everyone else, wanted to show proper respect to the anthem.

Le Petomane, modest man that he was, went back to baking at the outbreak of war in 1914, and just as there was no one like him before, there has been no one since. There was an imitator in 1900, a woman who made inroads before being revealed as a fraud. (She concealed a whoopee cushion in her skirt.) Still, the fact that someone would go to such lengths confirms yet again the magic appeal of the fart, and that whether or not we receive direction from Amy Vanderbilt or her professional colleagues, the magic will prevail, as it did long before humans learned to say, "Excuse me."

emerge informed

Is Mother Nature perverse or what? Lovebirds spend 99.9 percent of their mating time in foreplay. Lovebugs, on the other hand, get right to the point, so to speak, and stay there. The male spends its entire life span copulating. In the air! Yet, screwworms are impotent. Go figure.

Despite the *Four Seasons* and other huge successes, Antonio Vivaldi's career in Venice gradually began to slide, so in 1740 he left for Vienna, where Charles VI was one of his greatest admirers. Unfortunately, Charles sat down to a plate of bad mushrooms that year, so Antonio had to go looking again. Not for long, though. Vivaldi passed away in July of 1741, at age 63. At his funeral mass in the magnificent St. Stephen's Cathedral of Vienna, there was a nine-year-old boy soprano in the choir. His name was Franz Joseph Hayden.

The famous Smithsonian Institution, in Washington, D.C., was established by Congress in 1846 with £100,000 left by James Smithson (1765–1829), the illegitimate son of Hugh Smithson Percy, 1st Duke of Northumberland, and Elizabeth Macie. Smithson was a mineralogist. (Smithsonite, a.k.a. calamine, is named after him.) He never once set foot in the U.S.

Cicer is Latin for "chickpea." Also for "wart." Marcus Tullius Cicero had a prominent cicer on his nose, one reason his friends tended to call him Marcus Tullius rather than Cicero. *Cicer*, by the way, is fourth declension, neuter.

How the Olympics used to be: Canada and England were tied 9 to 9 for the gold in lacrosse (now discontinued) in 1908, when Canada's star, Frank Dillon, broke his stick. To keep the sides even, England's star, R. G. Martin, withdrew until a new stick could be found for Dillon. (Canada won 14 to 10.)

125

ken
WEBER

hands-free word adventure

Along the Eponymous Trail

P. T. Barnum's great elephant, Jumbo, did more than amaze people. (He passed on in 1885, but is still the largest elephant on record.) He also bequeathed his name for things that are truly big. Other, albeit smaller types, have done similarly. In 1880, for example, a group of Irish farmers refused to deal with Charles Boycott. Then there's Amelia Bloomer, who led a revolt against hoopskirts and horsehair crinolines, and General Henry Shrapnel who devised an exploding artillery shell. Come a little further down our eponymous trail, and figure out the surnames that fit.

Louis _____ (1822–95) gave us a word for this process that kills germs.

César _____ (1850–1918) built very swank hotels.

Antoine-Joseph (Adolphe) _____ (1814–94) jazzed up the music world with a single-reed wind instrument.

Franz _____ (1734–1835) was a doctor who used hypnotism extensively in his practice.

Dr. Joseph _____ (1738–1815) He didn't invent this scary device but, for humanitarian reasons, suggested it to Robespierre and his pals.

Rudolf _____ (1858–1913) The engine he invented is often hard to start, but that does not bother most manufacturers of big trucks.

John Loudon ___ (1756–1836) Before John's idea, the potholes were even worse!

Jean _____ (17th century) This French army officer developed marching drills and used his position to impose extremely strict discipline.

Vidkun _____ (1887–1945) This Norwegian lent his surname to the lexicon of treason.

Alessandro _____ (1745–1827) Although he spent much of his time studying swamp gas, he detoured into electricity too. His name is often seen in "Danger! 500 ____s!"

Answers on page 143

shifts of wit

You will feel sympathy for the predicament Tallulah Bankhead once faced. But who among us could respond with her sangfroid? Caught short in a toilet stall, having turned to the paper after the fact — as we all do — Tallulah rapped on the side of the cubicle to get the attention of an adjacent passenger. "Dahling," she said, "do you have two fives for a ten?"

Although it isn't a model of "cool," one of the irresistible entries in the Bankhead legacy is her remark to a priest at Midnight Mass.

"Dahling," she commented through the cloud of incense, "your gown is lovely but I'm afraid I have to tell you your purse is on fire."

Poet and radio star Franklin Pierce Adams (who liked to be referred to as FPA) was sitting beside Beatrice Kaufman (wife of George S.) at a cocktail party when her chair seat collapsed, leaving her stuck in the frame with her feet in the air. Into the complete silence that followed, Adams said sharply, "I've told you a hundred times, Beatrice, that's not funny!"

British writer Walter Savage Landor (1775–1864) more than substantiated his middle name with a lifetime of quarrels and explosions of temper. His cook once had the bad luck to serve a substandard meal to Landor when he was already having a bad day. Landor blew up, seized the tiny man by the scruff and belt, and threw him out the window into a flowerbed. The incident was no surprise to the household staff; it had happened before. But they were shocked that it happened on that particular spring day. So was Landor immediately after, for he ran to the window: "Good God!" He leaned out. "I forgot the violets."

The opening movement of Claude Debussy's *La Mer* has the subtitle "From Dawn to Noon at the Sea." Contemporary and fellow composer Erik Satie was at the premiere, and Debussy, quite naturally, asked him what he thought of it. "I quite liked the bit about quarter to eleven," Satie said.

Those who were there in 1933 swear this really did happen. James Barrie, author of *Peter Pan*, was seated beside G. B. Shaw at a dinner party, where Shaw's customary dish of greens and dressing was already served and waiting. "Tell me," he said to GBS, "are you going to eat that, or have you already?

going out in style ...more or less

One would think the literati always go out with panache. Yet, for people who supposedly live by the word, the exit lines of some professional writers have been remarkably ordinary.

A perfect example of that blandness comes from Matthew Arnold, poet and unofficial critic of absolutely everything in Victorian England. "The end," Arnold said as he breathed his last in 1888.

Fortunately for collectors of pre-mortem quips, Robert Louis Stevenson raised Arnold's departure profile with the following observation at the funeral: "Poor Matt. He's gone to heaven, no doubt. But he won't like God."

Somerset Maugham made a stab at irony when he went in 1965: "Dying is a very dull, dreary affair, and my advice to you is to have nothing whatever to do with it."

Maugham's observation was perhaps inspired by writer Lytton Strachey in 1932: "If this is dying then I don't think much of it."

There's some literary satisfaction from German poet Heinrich Heine (1856): "God will forgive me. It's His profession."

However, truly memorable departures on the part of the literati seem to be more a product of lifestyle than the verbal grace one might hope for. For example: "I've had eighteen straight whiskies. I think that is the record." That was Dylan Thomas in 1953. No surprise there — except that it was not a crafted line. He was into one of his regular drinking bouts at the time and not on a deathbed.

What may be a surprise is that Marcel Proust, on his last day in 1922, sent for — not champagne, but beer!

On the other hand, Anton Chekhov did have champagne. On doctor's orders! "I haven't had champagne for ages," he said as he drained his glass and expired, in 1904.

The champagne bon mot of them all, fittingly, is a final toast by Oscar Wilde, who was living in poverty in Paris and had contracted meningitis: "I am dying beyond my means." Another version of the quip is "I suppose I shall have to die beyond my means," spoken to a doctor who'd asked an exorbitant fee.

Outshining both of those, however, is another (probably apocryphal) Wilde exit line: "Either that wallpaper goes, or I do."

pen-free puzzle posers
(EASY)

1. The national flag of Kiribati is red with wavy blue and white lines at the base, and in the center, a golden rising sun and a frigate bird in flight. At the main government building in the capital, Tarawa, two members of the national police force (there is no army) stand guard from sunrise to sunset below the Kiribatan flag that flies at the front entrance.

When Kiribati became a republic in 1979 (it was formerly the Gilbert Islands) the commissioner of police resolved a protocol dilemma involving the guards. Military protocol demands that at the flag station, guards must face in opposite directions. Yet a traditional standard of politeness among the Gilbertese people requires that they must be able to see each other without turning around.

How did the Commissioner solve this dilemma?

2.   If you do this one right, you'll elicit the wrong answer from your subject well over half the time. Pose these questions to someone in rapid sequence.

Counting your thumb…

How many fingers on your right hand?

Your left hand?

On both hands?

On ten hands?

The answer you will get most of the time is "one hundred."

3.   After three years as a prisoner at the top of a secluded and long-abandoned lighthouse, Leiea was accustomed to the weekly bath routine. It was about the only diversion she looked forward to. A guard would lock her into a soundproof, windowless room where an old claw foot tub was already filling with hot water. Leiea would undress and put her clothes on the only piece of furniture in the small room, a rickety table in one corner. Beside it was a hook on which hung her change of clothing for the next week. Then she would have one hour to bathe and dress, after which the guards would return and take her away.

On the day of the crisis, Leiea's first thought was how, after three years, she had never before noticed the hole in the ceiling. Not a large one. Maybe the size of a golf ball. Had it been there all the time? She did not waste her time trying to remember. Without hesitation, Leiea stepped onto the edge of the tub. Her aim was to get onto the little table and hope it would hold her long enough to get a close look, but she never got that far. Her foot slipped, hit the faucet and broke it right off. Water gushed out, overflowed the tub and began to fill the tiny room. She yelled, but the guard was gone and wouldn't be back for an hour. Now what?

How did Leiea keep from drowning?

Answers on page 142

trivia test

Getting There Is Half the Fun

During the Seige of Khartoum in 1885, British commander Charles George "Chinese" Gordon held out for ten months while the War Department diddled over how, when, and even whether to relieve him and his very thin forces. When the pooh-bahs in London finally decided to do something, they hired the Thomas Cook travel agency to get the relief force down the Atlantic coast, across the Mediterranean, and up the Nile. The agency hired boatmen from across the Empire and booked a total of 1,505 boats, from liners to dories, to do the transport. They found their way, and they didn't lose the luggage. But they were two days late.

In what country would you be if:

1.   You were in the city of Tripoli?

2.   You were standing on the north magnetic pole?

3.   You were in the northernmost part of Scandinavia?

4.   The national flag is neither a rectangle nor a square?

5.   The Dominican Republic occupies the other half of the island?

6.   One of the four official languages is Romansh?

7.   In the Alps, the mountains have names like Koskiusko, Jagangul, Bogong and Feathertop?

8.   The capital city is San José?

9.   It has the only Great Lake entirely within its borders?

10.   Its borders touch every other country on its continent but two?

11.   Estonia is due east and Lithuania due west?

12.   You are standing at 51°N latitude and 0° longitude?

Answers on page 142

emerge informed

The three Wise Men (from the East) are Gaspar, Melchior and Balthazar. The three Wise Monkeys (from Japan) are Mizaru (see no evil), Mikazaru (hear no evil) and Mazaru (speak no evil). The three Stooges were Larry, Curly and Moe.

Rabbits and hares do not mate. (They don't even date.) Hares have longer ears and longer legs, but they have only half as many tastebuds, and are born with hair. Rabbits are born bald.

The first Crayola crayons came off the line in 1903 with eight colors, but makers Binney and Smith have been adding and subtracting ever since. They once got up to over 90, but since 1972, the company has maintained the number of colors at 72. In 1990 they took out maize, orange yellow, raw umber and five others, replacing them with eight new colors, including wild strawberry, cerulean and dandelion.

The length of the axle on Roman chariots was standardized well before the time of Julius Caesar at 4 feet 8 inches. That is now the width, known as "standard gauge," of North American and most European railroad tracks.

When the National Hockey League was formed in November 1917, 97 percent of the registered players came from Canada. When the calendar flipped in January 2000 that figure was 60 percent. The NHL began the new millennium with players from 19 countries, including Nigeria, South Africa and South Korea.

for deposit in your "one-up" account

Real Words That, Unfortunately, Have Fallen Out of Use (and Which, Therefore, Need You to Help Reintroduce Them)

blype: a piece of skin that peels off after a sunburn

carminative: that which produces gas in the intestine

coprolite: a fossilized turd

eruciformic: caterpillar-like; shaped like a caterpillar

feaguing: putting ginger up a horse's fundament to make him carry the tail high

humper's lump: a body part that swells as a consequence of carrying heavy things

illth: the opposite of wealth

merism: expressing the whole in two contrasting parts (for example, "head to foot")

pandiculate: to stretch and yawn at the same time

pessimal: yes, the opposite of optimal

loft: the springiness of a material that causes it to return to shape after it's squeezed

pissabed: a yellow flower growing amid grass (in Samuel Johnson's dictionary)

quatrassential: important, but not quite at the top (that is, not quite quintessential)

rectalgia: pain in the ass

schwa: the unpronounced quasi-grunt syllable in words (for example, "uh" in often)

swyve: Middle English verb for the act of copulation (used by Chaucer)

wox: a contented, half-asleep state; utter contentment

hands-free word adventure

In a crossword-puzzle lover's closet

Ever wondered about this? If you have a bunch of odds and ends in your closet, and you throw out all but one of them, what do you call it? For sure it's an "end" but what if it's a really odd "end"? A compromise word might be found in the Latin *residuum* (but then if you're one of those pack rats who just can't bear to clean out — as opposed to clean up — you'd have to go with *residua*).

Here are some interesting residua, truly odd ends that might be found in the closet of a crossword puzzle buff.

dottle   sabot   jess   dibble   kif
aglet   beson   pledget   ort   pintle

Match each object above with its proper description below. (Don't give up on this! Some of these you know. Some you can figure out logically. A few, we acknowledge, are just *residua*.)

a wooden shoe
a short pointed tool for making holes in the ground
a scrap of food (like a dried bread crust)
a leather leg strap on a falcon
a butt of Indian hemp (ready to light)
a metal or plastic shoelace end
a broom (usually a curling broom)
a wad of lint in your navel
a post that is part of a hinge
a plug of tobacco ash at the bottom of a pipe

Answers on page 143

pen-free puzzle posers
(CHALLENGE)

1. A quiet, unseen drama took place in the library at the Worthington-Smythe estate in Suffolk. Following a carefully outlined proscription common to all Victorian books of etiquette, Lady Worthington-Smythe had given firm instructions that never ever was a book by a male author to be shelved beside a book by a female author. Thus when her ladyship learned to her horror that George Eliot, the author of *Silas Marner*, was actually a woman, she decreed that the copy be re-shelved appropriately. Accordingly, *Silas Marner*, a special edition with vellum-wrapped covers eight millimeters thick, was stood to the immediate left of Charlotte Bronte's *Jane Eyre*, since this author too, published under a male pseudonym, Currer Bell. Both books are imposing tomes. *Jane Eyre* is also a special edition — its total page width is seven centimeters, just like Silas Marner, but with covers at five millimeters, it is somewhat thinner overall than its new shelfmate.

What neither Lady Worthington-Smythe nor the household staff knew, was that a very active bookworm was at work on the title page of *Silas Marner*, and by the time it was discovered, the worm had eaten its way through to the back page of *Jane Eyre*, ruining both books.

What distance had the bookworm covered between the time of the re-shelving and the time it was discovered?

2. What is the next number in this sequence? 77, 49, 36, 18, ___

3. As you emerge from a complex set of underground passages onto a barren plain with mountains barely discernible in the distance, you realize that your job as a guide is in jeopardy. You know that you are either in Lobo or Lupo, and you have to find out which. It's wonderful hiking country, but Lobans — and Lupans especially — are more than a bit weird. Citizens of both countries wear the same clothes, right down to their shoelaces. They can't be told apart. And their speech! They use only one-word sentences.

The hiking group behind you doesn't know much about this. They don't know where they are, and they don't really care. They assume you know. After all, it's your job.

All in all, a tight situation. Fortunately for the hikers, and for your job security, there is someone up ahead. It could be a Loban or a Lupan; you don't know. One thing you can count on, however. Lobans tell the truth. Always. And Lupans always lie. Without fail; they can't help themselves. Now, you know from experience that you'll be able to ask one and only one question.

What one question can you ask that will at least tell you where you are?

Answers on page 143

 trivia test

Playing the Game

When James Naismith from Almonte, Ontario, got the idea for a new indoor ball game in 1891, he called it "indoor rugby," even though the object was to put a soccer ball into bushel baskets at either end of the playing surface. Perhaps the name diverted attention from the inconvenience of trying to get the ball out of the baskets after a score. It wasn't until 1912 that baskets with open bottoms were made official. Before that, there was only a small hole in the bottom so the referee could use a stick to push the ball out the top!

1. Name twelve different competitive games played with a solid ball (that is, neither hollow nor inflated with air).

2. In what sport do you lose by accumulating the greatest number of points?

3. Had it not been for horses, this popular sport would likely never have developed. Yet, if they choose to, players do not have to take a horse out of its stable at any point during the game. What sport?

4. In major league baseball, what is the least number of pitches that the pitcher of the visiting team can throw in a game it loses?

5. The first Winter Olympics were held in Chamonix, France. In 1924? 1928? Or 1932?

6. John L. Sullivan won the heavyweight boxing title in 1892 (fighting bare-knuckled), held it for just under 11 years, then lost it to James J. Corbett (fighting with gloves). Who is the only fighter to hold the heavyweight title longer than Sullivan?

7. For 25 years, beginning in 1942, there were six teams in the National Hockey League. In 1967, six more joined. How many can you name?

8. No one before or since Canadian swimmer Cindy Nicholas has come even close to equaling her marathon feats. There is one body of water she crossed 19 times — across and back, 5 times! What body of water is that?

9. In what sport does Hervé Filion hold the world record for most victories? (Hint: He and his competitors always wear goggles.)

10. In what games do you (i) pot winks? (ii) make a cradle cannon? (iii) make a two-handed dead lift? (iv) play against your opponent in a fronton? (v) shoot a Portsmouth Round?

Answers on page 142

emerge informed

After the last helicopter lifted off the roof of the U.S. Embassy in Saigon in 1975, Muzak was still being piped throughout the building and the grounds.

"Put a sock in it!" A contemporary expression for "Shut up! Pipe down!"? Not really. Not contemporary, anyway. Early models of hand-cranked phonographs (remember the dog peering into the sound horn?) had no volume control, and the tinny sound often blared uncomfortably out of the horn. Listeners discovered they could mute the sound by stuffing the horn with a heavy woolen sock. Incidentally, the dog peering into the horn? His name was Nipper.

Throughout her career, Mae West never kissed a leading man on screen.

The "ring finger" comes from a Christian tradition in medieval Europe. The priest would touch the wedding ring to the bride's left thumb for God the Father, touch the index finger with it for Jesus Christ, and then the second finger for the Holy Spirit. The ring would then go on the third finger, showing, symbolically, the groom's order of priority: first, the three members of the Trinity, then, in fourth place, the wife.

Pythagoras (c. 530 B.C.) was responsible for the Pythagorean theorem. (The square of the length of the hypotenuse of a right-angled triangle, etcetera.) If you have forgotten this one, you might have an easier time remembering that Pythagoras avoided eating beans because he thought they made him lustful.

shifts of wit

If you are a politician and need votes, it is especially difficult to respond tactfully when someone asks for something you have neither the time nor the inclination to do. A model response might be available from Benjamin Disraeli (1804–81). A successful novelist before going into politics — he was prime minister twice — Disraeli thus attracted more than a few requests to read and express an opinion on unpublished manuscripts. His standard reply: "Thank you for the manuscript. I shall lose no time in reading it."

Hard to know what Disraeli would have thought of Albert Schweitzer's response when he was set upon by two elderly ladies on a train in Kansas.

"Have we the honor of speaking to Professor Einstein?" they wondered.

"No," Schweitzer answered, then added with supreme tact, "though I can quite understand your mistake. He has the same kind of hair I do. Inside our heads we're different, though." He smiled. "Still, we are very old friends. Would you like me to give you his autograph?"

Upon which, he tore a slip of paper from his notebook and inscribed, "Albert Einstein, by way of Albert Schweitzer."

Schweitzer's was a more creative, but not necessarily kinder, piece of tact than that of actor Marcello Mastroianni, who, realizing he was about to be presented with a gold watch by Joseph Levine, surreptitiously took off the gold watch he was already wearing and dropped it into a wastebasket.

Very often, a tactful response can be the product of a situation, even when tact is not normally found in the perpetrator. No better example than the Duke of Wellington. Under normal conditions, he was unimpeded by the presence of others he deemed inferior to himself, so that comments such as the following were his usual forte. When the idea of a public railway system was first broached to him in 1836, he immediately condemned the proposal, for it would, in his words, "cause the lower classes to move about."

awaiting your solution...

Don't Replace the Bagpipes!

28 May
To: Yvonne Hawkins, Claims
From: Eileen Cook, Investigations
Regarding: 42D1409 (Monk Transport/Agromax Inc./Green Fields)
See also: Highway Patrol incident report 22/05/00, Ref. 76A
Preliminary recommendations regarding claim of Roger Monk (comprehensive).

Mr. Monk is owner-driver of a diesel-powered, cab-over-engine, Freightliner tractor with rear tandem axle. Sleeper compartment in rear of cab. Trailer is flatbed type (24 feet) used for clean haul. Single rear axle. Complete equipment specifications for both tractor and trailer will be attached to final report.

On 22 May, at approximately 10 A.M , Mr. Monk drove his equipment to the entrance gate of Agromax Fertilizer Company. He acknowledges that he was aware that Agromax was then (and continues to be) the object of demonstrations by a citizens' group (Green Fields) opposed to the company's manufacturing practices. He further acknowledges that there have been a number of violent incidents associated with the demonstrations, and that he was aware of this before 22 May. It is Mr. Monk's contention that, since he is an independent operator, and has nothing to do with the practices of Agromax, he believed his scheduled pickup would take place without any difficulty.

Mr. Monk alleges that as he approached the gate (trailer was empty), the demonstrators set upon his equipment and caused the damage listed in his claim. Police report (see above for reference) confirms that every tire, excluding spares, was slashed; both exhaust stacks damaged; headlamp and clearance lights broken; windshield cracked; and exterior of cab scratched. Mr. Monk alleges further that a demonstrator got into his sleeper briefly during the melee. (Latter claim confirmed by Highway Patrol this date.)

Claim by Monk specifies as follows:

1. Towing charges
2. Repainting of tractor (complete)
3. Replace windshield
4. Replace exhaust stacks
5. Replace two headlamps and seven clearance lights
6. Replace one set of bagpipes (sic!)
7. Replace sixteen tires

Pending my final report, I suggest negotiations begin as follows.

1. Towing charges: Accept. Equipment could not be moved under power.
2. Repainting: Negotiate for 50 percent. Tractor is four years old and has not been repainted since new. Odometer at 22 May was 215,080 miles.
3, 4, 5. Windshield, stacks, lamps & lights. Accept.
6. Deny. No proof the damage to bagpipes was caused by demonstrators. Mr. Monk has not established that the instrument was even in the sleeper. It's my opinion we would be supported judicially here under the principle of fairness.
7. Tires. Deny until further notice. Suggest you give Monk benefit of the doubt, and an opportunity to amend this part of the claim. Either he has erred, or this is a rather clumsy attempt to defraud.

Final report will be submitted by 1 June.

EC

What is the nature of Mr. Monk's error, or possibly, fraud?

Solution on page 142

ken
WEBER

solutions/answers

Solution to "Don't Replace the Bagpipes"

Depending on the country, the equipment Mr. Monk owns is called a "tractor-trailer," a "semi" (semi-transport), or "articulated lorry." Whatever the name, it is the type of truck commonly seen on the highways of the world, on which the power part, the cab with engine and other appropriate equipment, pulls a detachable trailer.

Whether it's known as a tractor-trailer, semi, articulated lorry or even by another name, wherever it is in the world, it will not have 16 working tires. It will have 14 (as Mr. Monk's does) or variations by 4 above and below that. The smallest of these combinations have 10 tires. Most common in North America are 18, 22 and 26, although specialty haulers are seen with 30, 34, and even as many as 48 or 52!

Check next time you're on the highway (but only if someone else is driving!) The front axle of the tractor doing the pulling will have 2 wheels (tires). Every other axle on both truck and trailer will have 4, a pair at either end, so, excluding spares, you will see 10, 14, 18, 22 and so on. You won't see one with 16.

Answers to "A horse is a horse..."

1. Palomino 2. Richard III in the final battle of the War of the Roses. 3. *The Godfather* 4. 60 inches. A hand is 4 inches. 5. Four horses and riders per team, although it is played with three per team in smaller indoor arenas. 6. She was the first woman jockey in the Kentucky Derby. 7. Lemuel Gulliver in *Gulliver's Travels* 8. Gene Autry, Champion; Mickey Mouse, Horace Horsecollar; Robert E. Lee, Traveler; Zorro, Tornado; Dick Turpin, Black Bess; Dudley Do-Right, Horse; Dale Evans, Buttermilk; Ben Cartwright, Buck 9. Red in *The Red Pony* 10. Eliza Doolittle in *My Fair Lady*

Answers to "Getting There Is Half the Fun"

1. Libya 2. Canada 3. Norway 4. Nepal 5. Haiti 6. Switzerland 7. Australia 8. Costa Rica 9. U.S.A. 10. Brazil (The "two" are Chile and Ecuador.) 11. Latvia 12. England (Greenwich)

Answers to "Playing the Game"

1. Billiards (including snooker, skittles and pool); bowling (and lawn bowling); bocce; golf; baseball (including softball and slo-pitch); lacrosse (box and field); croquet; polo; hockey (field); handball; jai alai (aka pelota vasca); cricket. 2. Golf 3. Horseshoe pitching 4. [25] The home team hits a home run on the first pitch after which the visiting team pitcher throws three groundouts/flyouts. Four pitches for inning one, and three each for inning two to eight [4 + 3 x 7 = 25]. Home team doesn't bat in the ninth. 5. 1924 6. Joe Louis, 11 years, 8 months (June '37–March '49] 7. California Seals, Minnesota North Stars, Los Angeles Kings, Pittsburgh Penguins, Philadelphia Flyers, St. Louis Blues 8. English Channel 9. Harness racing 10. (i) tiddlywinks (ii) billiards (iii) weight-lifting (iv) jai alai (v) archery

Answers to "Pen-Free Puzzle Posers (Easy)"

At the government building in Tarawa, Kiribati, the guards face each other.

The answer you will get most of the time is 100; the proper response is 50.

Leiea pulled the plug.

Hands-Free Word Adventure: "In a crossword-puzzle lover's closet"

dottle, plug of tobacco ash; *aglet*, end of shoelace; *sabot*, wooden shoe; *beson*, a broom; *jess*, leather strap; *pledget*, wad of lint; *dibble*, pointed tool; *ort*, scrap of food; *kif*, butt of hemp; *pintle*, hinge post.

P.S. Here are some residua we couldn't work into this adventure, since even your closet would be an unlikely place for them. But if you love words, these are valuable additions to your vocabulary: *gruntle*, snout of a pig; *bort*, chips or dust left over when diamonds are polished; and *tittle*, the dot over the letter "i". It's just too unlikely that items such as these would be lying there in the *gnurr* (dust, lint, hair, etc. that gathers in corners — and in pockets and purses) with your other stuff.

Hands-Free Word Adventure: "Along the Eponymous Trail"

Louis *Pasteur*, pasteurization. César *Ritz*, ritzy. Antoine-Joseph *Sax*, saxophone. (He also invented the saxotromba, which, if you have ever heard one, proves there is a limit to musical ingenuity.) Franz *Mesmer*, mesmerize. Dr. Joseph *Guillotin*, guillotine. (The instrument, known by a variety of other names, had been used in Italy for centuries. The Guillotin family was so embarrassed when their name became associated that they changed it when Joseph died.) Rudolf *Diesel*, diesel. John Loudon *McAdam*, macadam — asphalt-paved road. Jean *Martinet*, martinet, for a person obsessed with authority. (His birth and death dates are unrecorded.) Vidkun *Quisling*, quisling. Alessandro *Volta*, volt.

Answers to "Pen-Free Puzzle Posers (Challenge)"

The bookworm travels 13 millimeters. It travels from the title page of *Silas Marner*, which stands on the left of *Jane Eyre*, through the former's front cover (8 mm) and then through the latter's back cover (5 mm).

The next number is 8. (7 x 7 = 49, 4 x 9 = 36, 3 x 6 = 18, 1 x 8 = 8)

Is this your country? If the individual is a Loban and if this is Lobo, the answer will be "Yes." If the individual is a Lupan and this is Lobo, the answer will be "Yes." If, however, this is Lupo, the truthful Loban will say "No," and the prevaricating Lupan will also say "No." Thus a "Yes" means you're in Lobo and a "No" means you're in Lupo, no matter what the undetermined nationality of the individual you have asked.

section SIX

emerge informed

Given that the Sioux were victors over Custer at the Little Big Horn (the nearby river in Montana), it's curious we don't call it the Battle of the Greasy Grass, for that was their name for the river. If you have your Custer file open, you likely know that he graduated bottom of his class at West Point, and that members of the Seventh Cavalry, not to mention some of his previous commands, were not always comforted by stories about their leader. One such, apparently true, was that Custer once shot his own horse while hunting buffalo!

The world's first commercially produced jockstrap jogged off the line in Guelph, Ontario, made by the Guelph Elastic Hosiery Company. Sociologists have yet to explain the significance of the fact that the world's first wire coat-hanger also came off the line in Guelph (albeit a different line) at about the same time.

Robin Williams had audiences laughing and crying with his portrayal of army radio disk-jockey Adrian Cronauer in *Good Morning, Vietnam!* However, the real Adrian Cronauer's voice can be heard blasting out "Good morning, Vietnam!" on the soundtrack of *Platoon*. This was not an inside joke. *Platoon* was released at least a year before the Robin Williams movie.

The shortest verse in the New Testament is John 11:35: "Jesus wept." There is no indication in the New Testament, in either short verse or long, that Jesus ever smiled.

shifts of wit

One of the more remarkable men of the nineteenth century was Sir Moses Montefiore. He distinguished himself in many ways, not least by living to the age of 101, and by being the only Jew born in Italy ever to be made a knight of the realm by Queen Victoria. Sir Moses was a tireless campaigner, in thought, word and deed, on behalf of Jews worldwide. One of the gems in the "word" category was delivered at a dinner party in London, where he had the bad (or good) fortune to be seated across from an anti-Semite who opened conversation by saying he had just returned from Japan where — most unusual — they don't have pigs and they don't have Jews!

"In that case," Sir Moses suggested, "you and I should go there so they will have a sample of each."

When the filming of *A Bill of Divorcement* (1932) was at last completed, Katharine Hepburn turned to her co-star, John Barrymore, with "Thank God, I don't have to act with you anymore."

To which Barrymore responded, "I didn't know you ever had, darling."

One of the patron saints in the world of wit is Lady Margot Asquith (1864–1945), who not only got off her share of bon mots (allegedly at Winston Churchill) but also caught a few in her time too. (A blue-ribbon example of the latter was in Dorothy Parker's review of Asquith's outspoken *Autobiography*. Parker said the affair between Margot Asquith and Margot Asquith was one of the prettiest love stories of all time.) However, the following incident suggests why Her Ladyship was very much someone to contend with.

When 1930s platinum-blonde movie star Jean Harlow was introduced to Dame Asquith, Harlow not only made the supreme gaffe of addressing her by first name, she also mispronounced it, saying Mar*got* (as in *got*).

Lady Asquith corrected her. "My dear, the *t* is silent, as in Harlow."

Bystanders were split about 50-50 over whether Harlow got it.

Prince Klemens von Metternich, who dominated the Congress of Vienna, the peace conference that followed the Napoleonic Wars, once complained to a British representative, Lord Dudley, that, "The common people of Vienna speak better French than the educated men of London."

"That may be so," Dudley answered, "but Your Highness will recall that Bonaparte has not been twice in London to teach them."

After 41 years of teaching English literature at Yale, William Lyon Phelps was not even mildly ruffled by this note at the bottom of a student's Christmas exam paper.

"God only knows the answer to this question," it said. "Merry Christmas."

"God gets an A," Phelps wrote. "You get an F. Happy New Year."

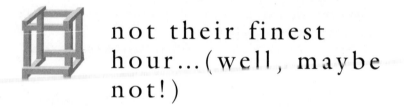

not their finest hour...(well, maybe not!)

According to J. V. Cosmon, in *A Funny Thing Happened on the Way to the Blackboard* (1972, self-published), these classroom malapropisms are "in the top 20:"

A gelding is a stallion with his tonsils taken out so he will have more time for himself. (fifth grade)

A monologue is a conversation between two people such as a husband and wife. (third grade)

From a Home Economics examination: "Is the Gibson Girl skirt worn above or below the ankles?" (From a ninth grader) Depends what the Gibson Girl is doing.

When Henry VIII died it took twelve men to carry the beer. (twelfth grade)

Donatello's interest in the female nude helped make him the father of the Renaissance. (college sophomore)

Mexico was conquered by Kotex. (fourth grade)

And herewith, from the files of the author of *The Toilet Papers,* never before published, more brilliance. All of these are by graduate university students who already held at least one degree:

On this issue, Prime Minister Laurier attempted to straddle the fence, and in doing so, lost his French support.

Out in the fields the peasants were starving, while, warm and comfortable in the palace at Versailles, Louis was holding his big balls.

After Duncan's death at the hands of Macbeth, his two sons fled to England and Ireland, respectively. This was not the last of the Scotch to go abroad.

In this, we must assume that God and not Becket is speaking, for God and Becket have now one will. Therefore it must be God's will that Becket become a martyr, not Becket's will attempting, however unintentionally, to direct God's will. (If you find this confusing, imagine what it must have been for Becket!)

trivia test

It's Dark in Here!

John, Paul and Ringo ranked the color black as one of life's true pleasures ("second only to steak and chips"!). The U.S. Mint chose a buffalo named Black Diamond to be the model for the U.S. nickel. Black stallions are popular, as are black sheep, blackjack dealers and black marketeers. There are Blackshirts, black belts, black widow spiders. There's even a Black Sea. (Okay, a red and a white one, too — and a yellow one and a dead one!) Nevertheless, there's a lot of this cheery dark color around.

1. What soccer player was called the "Black Pearl"?

2. What native people on the plains were mightier than the Sioux but decided against going to war during the settlement of the west?

3. When child movie star Shirley Temple Black returned to the public eye in adulthood, she did so as U.S. ambassador to what African country?

4. What terrorist organization recruits disillusioned Vietnam vet Bruce Dern to fire poison darts into the Super Bowl crowd in *Black Sunday*?

5. The 1919 Black Sox scandal saw the Chicago White Sox lose the World Series to whom?

6. True or false: the black snake is poisonous.

7. What was black about Edward "The Black Prince" (1330–76)?

8. In the first several years of the long-running TV show *Gunsmoke*, a regular character with a small role was Dodge City's blacksmith. What famous movie star played the role?

9. During what war did the incident known as "The Black Hole of Calcutta" take place: Sepoy Rebellion? Hundred Years War? Seven Years War?

10. Who recorded "The Man in Black" (also the title of his autobiography)?

11. Who played the role of Pussy Galore in the James Bond pic *Goldfinger*?

12. Beatles manager Brian Epstein discovered Priscilla White. She became famous as whom? ("You're My World" and other hits)

Answers are on page 167

this could take a minute, so be sure there's no one waiting

There Is No Greater Coincidence Than, Well, Coincidence!

On July 20, 1944, at precisely 12:36 P.M., Colonel Claus Count von Stauffenberg whispered to the officer next to him that he had an important telephone call to make, and then excused himself from the conference table at the Wolfschanze headquarters in East Prussia. On the floor, in von Stauffenberg's briefcase, was a bomb set to explode at 12:42 and eliminate Adolf Hitler. The Count had been seated to one side of the Führer, near the head of the table, and the briefcase was just a chair's width or two from him. Von Stauffenberg closed the door quietly behind him, and walked down the hall as quickly as dignity and the natural suspiciousness of the SS guards would allow.

But then: Coincidence? Destiny? Control by some force that is greater than us all? Natural course of human events? Or just plain bad luck? The officer the Count had spoken to seized the opportunity to make more room for his legs. It was, after all, a crowded table. He picked up the briefcase, momentarily surprised at how heavy it was, and then put it on the other side of a thick table support, giving himself considerably more space, and unwittingly saved Hitler's life. When the bomb went off — at 12:42 — it did so with devastating effect, but not the effect intended.

Forty-three years earlier, and not all that far away from what would one day be the Wolfschanze headquarters, coincidence — or human error — was also a factor, this time in sabotaging what should have been a successful flight by a flying machine. On Lake Tullnerbach, in Austria, on a warm October morning in 1901, a young piano-maker by the name of Wilhelm Kress had started the engine of his aircraft and was waiting for it to warm up. The airplane he'd so carefully designed and built was glistening in the early morning sunlight. He didn't know it at that moment, but the specifications of his craft matched almost all of those that were to be used successfully in a similar machine two years later, at a place in North Carolina called Kitty Hawk.

Kress should have flown that day but didn't. Although he couldn't tell from its appearance, the engine he'd received from the Benz company in Germany was not quite the one he'd ordered. He had specified a model that would deliver 40 HP. And though the one warming up now as the sun rose higher in the sky provided the power he needed, it was a heavier model than the one he'd asked for. The airplane taxied along the surface of Tullnerbach and then went down instead of up.

Coincidence? Human error? Human weakness? Luck? That certainly is one way to explain the synergy that seems to govern not only history, but our personal lives as well. Another powerful example of the phenomenon lies in the discovery — and the subsequent development — of vulcanized rubber. Two names we associate with the product are Goodyear and Goodrich. Charles Goodyear was a struggling inventor, and Dr. Benjamin Franklin Goodrich, a former Civil War surgeon turned businessman. The former made the discovery — by coincidence — and the latter was able to develop its potential — by coincidence.

Although rubber had been known of for some time (the Carib Indians gave rubber balls to Columbus in 1492), it had few practical applications until the time of Goodyear's efforts, because in its natural state, rubber is brittle when cold and gooey when hot. Goodyear believed that to make it useful, rubber needed to be "cured" in a manner similar to the way in which leather is tanned to make it pliable. He made that discovery late one night in 1839. Not in a planned, controlled, laboratory fashion, however. Working in the family kitchen, the seriously impoverished Goodyear was experimenting with various substances when he spilled a mixture of rubber and sulfur on the surface of the hot stove. The mixture melted into a blend, but he was either too busy or too preoccupied to clean it up, so it stayed there until the stove went out. Later, as he was cleaning up, Goodyear noticed that the mixture had congealed into a substance with more elasticity than he had yet seen. He nailed it to an outside door for the rest of the night, and found in the morning that it was still pliable. Even better, the mixture retained its integrity at room temperature and higher. Charles Goodyear had stumbled on "cured" (vulcanized) rubber.

Unfortunately, the world paid very little attention, and Goodyear spent the rest of his life fruitlessly trying to make something out of his discovery. When he died in 1860, deeply in debt, very few people knew about vulcanized rubber and even fewer cared, especially in the United States, which was becoming pretty much absorbed with splitting up into North and South. Not until 1870 did another coincidence intervene. In the winter of that year, B. F. Goodrich, who by this time had started his small rubber company in Akron, Ohio, watched a friend's house burn down one night because the fire department's leather hoses had split in the cold. The disaster made him think of an article Goodyear had written: *Gum-Elastic and Its Varieties.* Looking down at the useless leather firehoses, Goodrich could not help but imagine what might have happened if they had been made of pliable rubber. Six months later the Akron factory was turning out hoses. They were an immediate best-seller, as were the jar ring-rubbers, gaskets, and ringer rollers for washing machines the company also began to produce. Within six years, almost all the world's rubber products were vulcanized.

Was Goodyear jinxed and Goodrich blessed? Hard to know. Where does luck begin and end, and where does initiative and application take over? When does the who-you-know factor take over? Or the who-knows-you? Goodyear simply could not interest investors. Goodrich, on the other hand, brought a group of supporters on board with no effort at all. Was that luck or fate? Was Goodrich, but not Goodyear, in the right place at the right time, or did B.F. create the right place and right time by his own effort?

If you think luck or fate is always under your own control, try telling that to the innocent citizens of Peshtigo, Wisconsin. On the night of October 8, 1871, a forest fire roared out of the bush and utterly destroyed their community in minutes. There was no escape for the townspeople because the winds took the fire completely around as well as through the settlement. Survivors — only 500 out of a population of 2,000 — told how the river through town had actually boiled! The Peshtigo disaster got almost no publicity — then or since — and consequently, none of the assistance or support that publicity attracts because, coincidentally, October 8, 1871, was the same night a fire started in the O'Leary barn on De Koven Street in Chicago. The famous Chicago Fire was serious enough, but compared to what happened in Peshtigo, it was a mere fizzle.

One of the reasons that fate is often explained as an uncontrollable, even supernatural factor, is that after the event, especially if you look hard enough, it is often easy to identify elements that appeal to our natural human inclination to be teased by the possibility of the paranormal. The many comparisons in the assassinations of Abraham Lincoln and John F. Kennedy offer an easily understood example. Both presidents were civil-rights leaders; both suffered fatal head wounds; both were slain sitting beside their wives. Each was succeeded by a former senator from a southern state. Both successors were named Johnson. Both assassins were slain before coming to trial. John Wilkes Booth shot Lincoln in a theater and ran to a warehouse. Lee Harvey Oswald shot Kennedy from a warehouse and ran to a theater. Booth was born in 1839; Oswald in 1939. Lincoln's secretary (named Kennedy) advised against going to the theater, Kennedy's secretary (yes, named Lincoln!) advised against the convertible in Dallas. Although aficionados of this type of comparison often sink into the absurd (for example, both surnames have seven letters), there are so many points of similarity that to look beyond the physically normal to the psychically abnormal is almost irresistible.

But is it fair to the truth to do so? It is also possible to develop an equally long catalogue of differences. (Begin with the fact that Lincoln's son Robert Todd Lincoln was nearby when the president was shot. Robert Todd was also at hand for President James Garfield's assassination, and when McKinley was shot in 1901. He was not around for Kennedy's demise.) Still, even if a careful interlocking of facts can be explained, the pull toward a notion that somehow there is a "divinity that shapes our ends," is very powerful. Think of this. On June 28, 1914, Crown Prince Ferdinand was shot in Sarejevo, thus launching what became the bloodiest military conflict the world has yet known. On that very same day, at Tobolsk, in Imperial Russia, a peasant woman tried, but failed, to kill "mad monk" Gregory Rasputin. What might have happened in our world if she had succeeded and Ferdinand's assassin had failed?

emerge informed

The seventh grade in St. Agnes School in Arlington, Massachusetts, developed a hypothetical stock portfolio in 1990–91 that produced a 70-percent gain over the next two years. Over that time, the grade seven kids' portfolio outperformed 99.1 percent of all North American equity mutual funds.

In Henry Cockeram's *The English Dictionarie* of 1623, *commotrix* is defined as "a Maid that makes ready and unready her Mistress." Ready or unready for what is not explained.

Fact: Archduke Franz Ferdinand bled to death after being shot at Sarejevo on June 28, 1914. Fact: The Archduke was an extremely vain man who regularly had the help sew him into his uniform for major occasions (such as Sarejevo). Fact: After the shooting, attendants couldn't get at the wound because the uniform was too tight and there were no buttons. By the time any one could find scissors, it was too late.

June 9 (1934) is Donald Duck's birthday. (It's Cole Porter's too — in 1893.) Included in Donald's curriculum vitae is an honorary doctorate from Yale: Doctorate of International Friendship, awarded in 1939. In 1970, Donald appeared on a San Marino postage stamp. For those who wonder about his exceptionally paternal relationship with nephews Huey, Dewey and Louie, their mother, Dumbella (Donald's sister), actually gave him custody of the three in a 1938 movie cartoon called, appropriately enough, "Donald's Nephews."

If two competitors sat down to play dominoes, and faithfully completed four games a minute, they would exhaust all possible combinations of the game in only 118 million years.

hands-free
word adventure

Find the money; it's there

No matter how perceptive or persistent you are, you will never find an egg in an *eggplant*, or ham in a *hamburger*. And you probably learned long ago to live with the fact that there is neither pine nor apple in a *pineapple*. To compensate, however, there is *cash* to be found in a sentence such as "In his left hand, Lu*cas h*eld a bottle"; *money* in the sentence "He'd hit botto*m one y*ear after Mona left"; and even foreign currency in "He knew now she was *som*ewhere in Uzbekistan." (Okay, maybe you didn't know the basic currency unit of Uzbekistan is the *som*, but you get the idea.)

Delve a little further into Lucas's problem and see if you can find eleven different currencies. There's money from England, Italy, Germany, Korea, Albania, Sweden, France, Saudi Arabia, Mexico, South Africa, Japan (in that order):

To compound his woes, Lucas had learned he'd been looking for Mona in all the wrong places. Although he'd thought to call Ira, her twin brother from Arkansas, Ira was nowhere to be found either. Later, Lucas wondered why he'd even bothered. Unlike Mona, Ira was a trifle kooky. Not one to leave a trail either, even though Lucas did hear about him from a mutual friend in Akron, and sometime later, picked up a rumor about his being off ranching somewhere in the Peace River district of Alberta. It took a while before Lucas eventually realized that this trial, this search for Mona, was going to be his, and his alone. That's when he began to drink. Although he'd never been a boozer or even inclined to mope, solutions just seemed to elude him. That was what was so frustrating. Over and over he told himself he just had to find her, to look her in the eye, not in anger but in apology. To explain face to face why now, at last, he knew he'd been wrong. So terribly wrong.

Answers on page 167

shifts of wit

On a September day in 1948, a little boy nudged Pablo Picasso awake on the beach at Nice, in France. He held a piece of paper, and though the boy was too young to have even the foggiest idea who he was pestering, it was obvious to Picasso he'd been dispatched to get an autograph. (Just days before, a postcard that Picasso mailed to a friend had fetched over $30,000.) After a few seconds of annoyance at being awakened, Picasso took the paper from the little boy, tore it up, and then drew some designs on the boy's bare back. He then signed his name in his classic style and sent the boy back to his parents.

Composer Aaron Copland watched a fellow customer in a bookstore in Boston as she selected a copy of his *What to Listen for in Music*, along with a paperback copy of Shakespeare's *Twelfth Night*. As the woman approached the cash register, he stopped her and asked, "Would you like me to autograph your book?" She smiled weakly at him and said, "Which one?"

British publisher John Murray was inordinately proud of a handsome leather-bound Bible he'd received from the poet Lord Byron. Murray always kept this Bible in obvious view on a table in his foyer, until the day a visitor pointed out a handwritten scribble in John 18:40. In the sentence "Now Barabbas was a robber," Byron had deleted "robber" and inserted "publisher."

Norman Mailer was disappointed that William F. Buckley had not written something personal on the flyleaf of his new book when he sent the novelist a copy. Responding to the vanity that fills all writers, Mailer then turned to the index to see if he was cited in the book. There, beside Mailer's name, Buckley had written "Hi!"

ken
WEBER

Shortly before he died in 1971, Ogden Nash received a copy of one his works that had been out of print for some time. With the copy was a letter from a fan, Tom Carlson, who explained that he had once owned a copy of this book, autographed by Nash, but that his dog had chewed it up. The letter went on to say how difficult it had been to find another copy, and would Nash mind autographing once more? Only days later, Carlson got the replacement copy back in the mail, with the inscription: "To Tom Carlson or his dog — depending on whose taste it best suits, Ogden Nash."

At a recital he gave at a small Midwestern university where facilities were limited, baritone Robert Merrill found himself using a biology lab as a dressing room. At intermission he was relaxing there when a student used a passkey to get in. "I never sign autographs at intermission!" Merrill declared, more than a little miffed at her boldness.

"I don't want your autograph," she said. "I've got to feed my snake."

pen-free puzzle posers
(MODERATE)

1. Seven inmates in Unit 12 on Devil's Island planned to escape by tunneling past a guard tower into the bushes. By sticking rigorously to a careful plan, they were able to tunnel at the rate of 4 yards a night. What the prisoners failed to account for, and why the guards were not terribly bothered by the possibility their charges might dig tunnels, was that the soft ground on the island was known to be unstable for tunneling. On a regular basis, 75 percent of the prisoners' nightly burrowing would collapse the next day and have to be re-tunneled. They were a persistent group, however, and one night made it out. In the investigation that followed, the inspector-general of prisons was told that the tunnel was only 16 yards long. *For how many nights did the prisoners have to dig?*

2. Boston Mills Steel-Press has just received a rush order for 300 tons of a cold rolled alloy in which they specialize. It has come from their best customer in Argentina and specifies the steel be delivered in sheets one millimeter thick. At Boston Mills, sheet-steel production is accomplished by running bars through a succession of roller presses until the desired thickness is obtained. However, the minimum width their roller presses will adjust to is two millimeters.

The order was filled, nevertheless. *How was the specified thickness obtained?*

3. The weather girl smiled at the TV camera, confident that her audience, even if it had only minimal interest in meteorology, would at the very least pay careful attention to the length of her skirt.

"You probably noticed," she began with a knowing smile, "that today's weather has been quite different from yesterday's." She turned slowly toward the electronic map and then returned to the camera. "Now as for tomorrow, if the weather is the same as it was yesterday, the day after tomorrow will have the same weather as the day before yesterday. But if the weather tomorrow is the same as today, the day after tomorrow will have the same weather as yesterday."

The smile widened. "As you know, it has been raining all day today, and it rained on the day before yesterday…"

At this point, the operators of cameras 1 and 2, who had both been slowly dollying in toward the weather girl's skirt, ran into each other and caused a short circuit that took the station off the air.

Was it raining or clear yesterday?

Answers on page 168

going out in style: a grave sense of humor

From an Edinburgh, Scotland, cemetery

> Beneath this stone,
> a lump of clay,
> Lies Uncle Peter Dan'els.
> Too early in the month of May
> Took off his winter flannels.

From Glasgow

> Here beneath this stone we lie,
> Back to back my wife and I.
> When the angels trump doth trill
> If she gets up then I'll lie still.

And this from Aberdeen

> Here lie the bones
> of Elizabeth Charlotte
> Born a virgin, died a harlot.
> She was aye a virgin at 17,
> A remarkable thing in Aberdeen.

Not hard to figure out that men were in charge of the grave-marker business...

Ribbesford, England, c. 1780

> The children of Israel
> wanted bread
> The Lord he sent them manna
> But this good man
> he wanted a wife
> And the devil sent him Ana

Hatfield Mass., 1771

> Here lies as silent clay
> Miss Arabella Young
> Who on the 21st of May
> Began to hold her tongue

Even a poet laureate got into the act. John Dryden (c. 1690) for his wife, Elizabeth Howard

> Here lies my wife.
> Here let her lie.
> Now she's at rest,
> And so am I.

Gone, but not forgotten, even if it takes poetic license...

From Skaneatles, New York

> Underneath this pile of stones
> Lies all that's left of Sally Jones
> Her name was Briggs,
> it was not Jones
> But Jones was used
> to rhyme with stones

Unknown, Texas

> Here lies John Bun
> He was killed by a gun
> His name was not Bun,
> but Wood
> But Wood would not rhyme
> with gun
> (but Bun would)

trivia test

Great Dates

The calendar we use in most of the western world (and in all the world, for commercial purposes) first went into general use in the final years of the sixteenth century. It replaced the Julian calendar, which by the year 1752 (using our calendar) was about 11 days out of whack. Our calendar begins at what is believed to be the year of Jesus Christ's birth. Everybody knows that. What everybody doesn't know is that the old Julian calendar used the founding of the city of Rome as its starting point. In our calendar, that's 753 B.C.

1. The old calendar was the Julian. What's ours called?

2. After whom was the Julian calendar named?

3. Father Hennepin first saw Niagara Falls in 1678. Since that year, how many years in our calendar read the same upside down and right side up?

4. In what century did
    (a) Jesse James's brother Frank die peacefully in his sleep?
    (b) Henry VIII have Anne Boleyn executed?
    (c) William Roentgen discover X-rays?
    (d) The last dodo bird die on the island of Mauritius?
    (e) Louis Braille develop his alphabet for the blind?
    (f) Edmond Halley observe the comet that bears his name?
    (g) "After the Ball," the first million-seller song (in sheet music), make it to the market?
    (h) Anton van Leeuwenhoek first describe human sperm as it appears under a microscope?
    (i) The Japanese fleet destroy the Russian Baltic fleet at Tsushima
    (j) Regular mail service begin between Canada and the U.S.?

ken
WEBER

5. Match the event in the left column, with the correct date in the right.

   (a)   Leonardo da Vinci completes the *Mona Lisa*.   1990
   (b)   Shakespeare is born.   1906
   (c)   Korean War ends in a truce.   1534
   (d)   Berlin Wall torn down.   1564
   (e)   The term *allergy* is first used in medicine.   1953
   (f)   Kodak introduces Photo CD (digital cameras).   1957
   (g)   Jacques Cartier sails down St. Lawrence River.   1989
   (h)   *West Side Story* premieres in New York.   1504

Answers on page 167

emerge informed

In 1977 the U.S. National Highway Safety Administration ordered the recall of more American-made cars than were built in that year.

The kind of pipe associated with Sherlock Holmes is a Calabash pipe. (It has nothing to do with Jimmy Durante's sign-off phrase, "Good night, Mrs. Calabash, wherever you are!" She ran a restaurant in Calabash, North Carolina, where Jimmy had lunch one day.) Holmes, in the Conan Doyle originals, never used such a pipe. American actor William Gillette adopted the Calabash — and the deerstalker hat — while portraying Holmes on stage, and the image struck a chord in the public's fancy.

Why you should never say "never again." The winner of England's Grand National Steeplechase in 1908 was a horse named Rubio. He went off at odds of 66 to 1, almost completely ignored by bettors because they knew he'd been retired from racing for three years and in the interim had been enjoying a career as a plow horse.

Saskatchewan gets the nod for most-difficult-to-pronounce (let alone spell) Canadian province. Easier than its Cree origin, though: *ksiskat-chewanisipi,* which means "fast-flowing river." Still, "Saskatchewan" doesn't pose the problem the whole country would have had if suggestions to replace the name "Canada" at Confederation in 1867 had been adopted. Samples — proposed quite seriously — Tuponia, Mesopalagia, Efisga and Albionora.

for deposit in your "one-up" account

Questions to ensure you'll be left alone.*

Who painted the floor of the Sistine Chapel?

Can a skunk gross out another skunk?

When the swallows come back to Capistrano...where have they been?

Wild Bill Hickok was shot holding the "dead man's hand": black aces and black eights. He was playing five-card draw, so what was the fifth card?

What is the number just before infinity?

Who was the first of the Mohicans?

What's the difference between a goblin and a hobgoblin?

What's the speed of dark?

Are there ovary whales?

Okay, Stanley said, "Doctor Livingstone, I presume?" What did Livingstone say?

What do you call virgin olive oil the next morning?

*These work best when offered spontaneously and completely out of context.

hands-free
word adventure

Anagrams at the Strip Mall

Writers write, in the English language, and manufacturers manufacture. But, strangely, grocers don't groce, fingers don't fing, and if you ever notice a lever leving it's not likely anyone will believe you (even though believers do believe).

Here are some doers who do. What you are offered is their names. Your task is to shuffle the letters of their names until you discover just what it is that they do. Brian Rial, for example, is a librarian, while Rosa Taunt is an astronaut.

These people helped build a strip mall. What do they do?

Merl Pub   Peter Cran   Kirby Clear   Chet Citar   Sam No

It wasn't long before the retail spaces in the mall were rented out. These are the people who took leases. What do they do?

Sherri Dares   Art Oil   Herb Cut   Rolf Sit   Mark E. Hose

At the south end of the mall, the builders put up a small professional building. The following took office space. (Anne Riviter took the whole bottom floor.)

Sue R. Nog   Sid Tent   Anne A. Riviter   Sue Seams   Anna C. Cutto

Answers on page 168

pen-free puzzle posers
(CHALLENGE)

1. Residents of Ballinafad have found they don't really need bed-side clocks with a face that glows at night. That's because the village clock not only *bongs* the appropriate number of times on the hour, it also strikes a single *bong* every quarter hour. When a resident of Ballinafad awakens in the darkness of the night (there are no streetlights, either) he or she has only to wait for a certain number of *bongs* to figure out what time it is.

What is the longest time a resident of Ballinafad might have to wait, in darkness, until he or she can be sure of the correct time?

2. You have a number of coins in your purse or pocket, none of which is larger than a quarter. *What is the greatest number of these coins that you can have and still not be able to make change for a dollar?*

3. There are three children in the Church family, the oldest being Lena. She is 17. Her sister, Mary Louise, was born seven years after their brother, Sterling. Two years ago, Lena was three times the age of Mary Louise.

How old will Sterling be when Mary Louise is as old as Lena is now?

Answers on page 168

trivia test

A Warm Fire, a Cold Winter Night, and a Real Page-Turner

Talk about "when you're hot, you're hot." Daniel Dafoe — and his publisher, as well — were completely surprised by the thumping success of *The Life and Strange Surprising Adventures of Robinson Crusoe, of York, the Mariner* when it hit the booksellers in 1719. Naturally, the publisher was anxious to follow up and Dafoe was more than willing to oblige. In only six weeks he finished *The Further Adventures of Robinson Crusoe*. It was a total bust with both critics and book buyers.

1. Name the novels in which these captains are found.

    Captain Queeg alienates the crew.
    Captain Flint sits on Long John Silver's shoulder.
    Captain Nemo is in charge of the sub.
    Captain Marlow learns that "Mistah Kurtz. He dead!"

2. Animals can be prominent in novels: match each name with its description.

    Ginger   Paddy   a no-name   Napoleon   Buck
                             hound

    (a) led an animal revolution down on the farm
    (b) won a sled-pulling contest in the Yukon
    (c) lived in a dreary, inaccessible swamp
    (d) was a dear friend of Black Beauty
    (e) dammed up Laughing Brook (upsetting Joe Otter and others)

3. Working at very top speed, who

    Wrote *She* in six weeks? (It did better than Dafoe's sequel)
    Wrote *Eight Cousins* in six weeks? (Off the morphine, too.)
    Wrote *Goodbye Mr. Chips* (an international hit) in four days?

4. Where, in Peru, is the bridge that Thornton Wilder wrote about? Where, in Burma, is the bridge that Pierre Boulle wrote about? Where, in Korea, are the bridges that James Michener wrote about?

5. In a classic French tale, the man in the iron mask at a secluded prison is an identical twin brother. Whose twin?

6. What is memorable in Walter Lord's *A Night to Remember*?

7. What uncomplimentary label does Katharine Anne Porter give the passengers of the luxury liner she wrote about in 1962?

Answers on page 167

shifts of (sports) wit

Football announcer Mike Ditka, on colleague John Madden: "He's one man who never let success go to his clothes."

Famed Yankee announcer, Mel Allen to a university conference: "I did pass the bar — and as some have argued, I've never passed one since!"

American boxer Bruce Selden, appearing on Japanese television, was asked, "What do you have to say to the people of Japan?" His answer: "I love Chinese food."

Clemens Westerhof, coach of the Nigerian World Cup soccer team after a resounding defeat: "It's not the sex that tires out young footballers. It's staying up all night looking for it."

Former Toronto Maple Leaf owner Harold Ballard, on a forward from Sweden whose style of play was not to his taste: "That guy could go into a corner with a dozen eggs and come out with the shells unbroken."

Professional golfer Lee Trevino, after a particularly poor day at the Masters: "If you are caught on a golf course during a storm and are afraid of lightning, hold up a one-iron. Not even God can hit a one-iron.

Joe Louis was once knocked down by a surprise left from Tony Galento, and was back on his feet before the count even started. After the round he was scolded by his trainer for getting up so fast. "What," Louis growled, "and let him get all that rest?"

Jimmy Quinn, manager of the Reading football club, on the many injuries suffered by his goalkeeper, Bobby Mihailov: "The only thing he hasn't had is mad cow disease."

R. J. Reynolds Tobacco Company paid Amelia Earhart to take several cartons of Lucky Strikes with her when she took off to fly around the world in 1937.

Quite understandably, Queen Victoria had never heard of Oxford math lecturer Charles Lutwidge Dodgson until she encountered him in his Lewis Carroll persona, and read all about the charming adventures of his heroine, Alice. The good queen wrote to him, told him how much she had enjoyed the book, and would he please send her something else he had written. He sent her a geometry text.

Hard not to be sympathetic with the feminist movement when it comes to medical training practices. The first woman doctor in Peel County, Ontario, for example, got her medical degree at University of Toronto in 1890. At the graduation ceremonies she was made to wait in the cloakroom until the male graduates received their degrees! This type of thing had been going on a long time. In the fourth century B.C., the city-state of Athens passed an ordinance outlawing women doctors.

For students of the deliciously arcane: When the former Edward VIII (later, Duke of Windsor) arrived back in England in 1937 with his June bride, Wallis Warfield Simpson, the train puffing into Victoria Station was being driven (as a royal treat) by Boris III, the king of Bulgaria.

According to Jack Warner of Warner Bros., the studio was never averse to sound dubbing, because actors and actresses, though they may be right for a part, don't always sound right. Which may explain why the studio regularly dubbed Rin Tin Tin.

solutions/answers

Answers to "It's Dark in Here"

1. Pélé 2. Blackfoot 3. Ghana 4. Black September 5. Cinncinati Reds 6. False. The black *mamba* is poisonous but not the "black snake." 7 His armor 8. Burt Reynolds 9. Seven Years War (1756–63) 10. Johnny Cash 11. Honor Blackman 12. Cilla Black

Answers to "Great Dates"

1. Gregorian, after Pope Gregory XIII (1572-85) 2. Julius Caesar 3. Three: 1691, 1881 & 1961. 4. (a) 20th (1915) (b) 16th (1536) (c) 19th (1895) (d) 17th (1681) (e) 19th (c.1840) He adapted a night cipher system that had been invented by a member of Napoleon's staff fifty years before. (f) 17th (c. 1676) (g) 19th (1894) (h) 17th (1677) (i) 20th (1905) (j) 18th (1792) 5. (a) 1504 (b) 1564 (c) 1953 (d) 1989 (e) 1906 (f) 1990 (g) 1534 (h) 1957

Answers to "A Warm Fire..."

1. Wouk: *The Caine Mutiny;* Stevenson: *Treasure Island;* Verne: *20,000 Leagues Under the Sea;* Conrad: *Heart of Darkness* 2. (a) Napoleon, in Orwell's *Animal Farm* (b) Buck, in London's *Call of the Wild* (c) the hound, in Doyle's *The Hound of the Baskervilles* (d) Ginger, in Sewell's *Black Beauty* (e) Paddy (the Beaver) in *The Adventures of Paddy the Beaver,* part of the Thornton W. Burgess animal series. 3. H. Ryder Haggard (of *King Solomon's Mines* fame) wrote She; Louisa May Alcott (of *Little Women*) wrote *Eight Cousins;* James Hilton (of *Lost Horizon*) wrote *Goodbye Mr. Chips.* 4. Wilder, at San Luis (Rey); Boulle, over the River Kwai; Michener, at Toko-Ri. 5. Louis XIV 6. The sinking of the *Titanic* 7. Fools, in her novel S*hip of Fools.*

Answers to "Hands-Free Word Adventure: Find the money; it's there"

England, pound; Italy, lira; Germany, mark; Korea, won; Albania, lek; Sweden, krona; France, franc; Saudi Arabia, rial (also riyal); Mexico, peso; South Africa, rand; Japan, yen.

To com*pound* his woes, Lucas had learned he'd been looking for Mona in all the wrong places. Although he'd thought to cal *Ira*, her twin brother from *Ark*ansas, Ira was nowhere to be found either. Later, Lucas *won*dered why he'd even bothered. Unlike Mona, Ira was a trif*le* kooky. Not one to leave a trail either, even though Lucas did hear about him from a mutual friend in A*kron, a*nd sometime later, picked up a rumor about his being of*f ran*ching somewhere in the Peace River district of Alberta. It took a while before Lucas eventually realized that this t*rial,* this search for Mona was going to be his, and his alone. That's when he began to drink. Although he'd never been a boozer or even inclined to mo*pe, so*lutions just seemed to elude him. That was what was so frustrating. Ove*r and* over he told himself he just had to find her, to look her in the e*ye, n*ot in anger but in apology. To explain face to face why now, at last, he knew he'd been wrong. So terribly wrong.

Answers to "Hands-Free Word Adventure: Anagrams at the Strip Mall"

Merl Pub is a plumber, Peter Cran a carpenter, and Kirby Clear a bricklayer. Chet Citar was the architect, and Sam No, a mason.

Sherri Dares rented space; she's a hairdresser. Art Oil's a tailor, Herb Cut a butcher. Rolf Sit is a florist and Mark E. Hose is a shoemaker.

In the professional building, veterinarian Anne E. Riviter rented, along with Sue R. Nog and Sid Tent, a surgeon and dentist, respectively. The masseuse, Sue Seams, thought it was ideal being on the same floor as the accountant, Anna C. Cutto.

Answers to "Pen-Free Puzzle Posers (Moderate)"

The prisoners tunneled for 13 nights. For the first 12, they dug 4 yards a night but 3 yards (75 percent) always caved in so they gained one yard a night, or 12 yards. On the 13th night, 4 yards of tunneling got them to the open air. Once they were out, it did not matter to them whether or not 75 percent of the 13th effort collapsed on the following day.

Boston Mills Steel-Press rolled two 2-millimeter sheets through together.

The weather was clear yesterday.

Answers to "Pen-Free Puzzle Posers (Challenge)"

The longest time a Ballinafad resident would have to wait is one and a half hours. If the first *bong* heard happens to be the one at 12:15 A.M., then there is no certainty of the time until 1:45 A.M. The longest series of single *bongs* (seven) occurs over this time-frame: 12:15 A.M. to 1:45 A.M.

In your purse or pocket: three quarters, four dimes, four pennies.

Sterling will be 24. Right now, when Lena is 17, Sterling is 14 and Mary Louise is 7.